18·95

# MAKING MANAGEMENT DEVELOPMENT WORK

THE BUSINESS OF TRAINING
Achieving Success in Changing World Markets
Trevor Bentley          ISBN 0-07-707328-2

EVALUATING TRAINING EFFECTIVENESS
Translating Theory into Practice
Peter Bramley          ISBN 0-07-707331-2

DEVELOPING EFFECTIVE TRAINING SKILLS
Tony Pont          ISBN 0-07-707383-5

DEVELOPING EFFECTIVE TRAINING SKILLS
Tony Pont          ISBN 0-07-707383-5

MANAGING PERSONAL LEARNING AND CHANGE
A Trainer's Guide
Neil Clark          ISBN 0-07-707344-4

HOW TO DESIGN EFFECTIVE TEXT-BASED OPEN
LEARNING: A Modular Course
Nigel Harrison          ISBN 0-07-707355-X

HOW TO DESIGN EFFECTIVE COMPUTER BASED
TRAINING: A Modular Course
Nigel Harrison          ISBN 0-07-707354-1

Details of these and other titles in the series are available from:

The Product Manager, Professional Books, McGraw-Hill Book Company (UK) Limited, Shoppenhangers Road, Maidenhead, Berkshire, SL6 2QL. Telephone: 0628 23432 Fax: 0628 770224

# Making management development work

Achieving success in the nineties

**Charles Margerison**

McGRAW-HILL BOOK COMPANY

**London** · New York · St Louis · San Francisco · Auckland
Bogotá · Caracas · Hamburg · Lisbon · Madrid · Mexico · Milan
Montreal · New Delhi · Panama · Paris · San Juan · São Paulo
Singapore · Sydney · Tokyo · Toronto

Published by
McGRAW-HILL Book Company (UK) Limited
Shoppenhangers Road, Maidenhead, Berkshire, SL6 2QL, England.
Telephone 0628 23432
Fax 0628 770224

---

**British Library Cataloguing in Publication Data**
Margerison, Charles J.
  Making management development work.
  1. Managers. Training.
  I. Title
  407.124

  ISBN 0-07-707382-7

**Library of Congress Cataloging-in-Publication Data**
Margerison, Charles J.
  Making management development work: achieving success in the
  nineties / Charles J. Margerison.
      p.  cm. — (The McGraw-Hill training series)
  Includes bibliographical references and index.
  ISBN 0-07-707382-7 (pbk.)
    1. Assessment centers (Personnel management procedure)  2. Career
  development. 3. Executive ability—Evaluation.  I. Title.
  II. Series.
  HF5549.5.A78M34  1991
  650.14—dc20

12345 BP 94321

Typeset by Book Ens Limited, Baldock, Herts
Printed and bound in Great Britain by The Bath Press, Avon

To
**GORDON WILLS**

**for his innovative, entrepreneurial, academic and personal contributions to helping myself and others advance on the management development highway**

# Contents

Preface                                                          xi
About the author                                                 xiii
Series preface                                                   xv
About the series editor                                          xvii

1   What is management development?                              1
    Who is going to succeed?                                     1
    Tradesmen and managers                                       2
    The continuum of management development                      2
    What is management development?                              3
    Managing improvement                                         4
    Guidelines                                                   5

2   Management development as a competitive weapon               7
    Problems as development opportunities                        7
    Taking risks                                                 8
    Managerial support                                           8
    How to get management development on track                   9
    A business view                                              11
    Management development and the corporate culture             13
    Guidelines                                                   13

3   Improving and reviewing performance                          15
    Describing performance accurately                            15
    Positive feedback                                            16
    Team building—improving teamwork                             16
    The team appraisal workshop                                  18
    The value of team appraisal                                  21
    Guidelines                                                   22

4   Management development and added value                       24
    What is the value of management development?                 24
    Outputs as a priority                                        24
    Executive education in major corporations                    25
    Small business for management development                    26
    Business responsibility                                      27
    The playing field                                            27
    Guidelines                                                   28

5   **What do managers want from management development?**        30
    Develop terms of reference                                   30
    Assumptions, prejudices and hypotheses                       33
    Why managers leave                                           33
    What makes a manager?                                        34
    Approaches to management development                         35
    Guidelines                                                   35

6   **How to learn from action**                                 37
    Learning from action                                         37
    Illustrations of action learning                             40
    The basis of managerial learning                             41
    How managers learn from experience                           42
    Reflecting on experience                                     43
    Guidelines                                                   44

7   **How to make career choices**                               45
    The key factors                                              45
    Personal experiences                                         46
    Making career choices—options                                47
    Early job experiences                                        49
    Assessing action levels                                      50
    Management education and development                         51
    Guidelines                                                   51

8   **Colleagues, managers, customers and competitors—keys to
    development**                                                53
    Ways we can learn from colleagues                            53
    Manage the experiences                                       55
    Learning areas                                               55
    Guidelines                                                   60

9   **Individual development plans**                             61
    Personal responsibility                                      61
    Development plans                                            61
    Self-development                                             63
    How often should you change jobs?                            63
    Changing roles                                               64
    Representing the organization                                66
    External development                                         67
    Management development and acting                            68
    Guidelines                                                   70

10  **Do you have any movers and shakers?**                      71
    High-energy people                                           71
    Assessment or development centres                            73
    Women in management                                          74
    Competition and cooperation                                  74
    Limited risks                                                75
    The Executive Connection                                     75
    Retaining the movers and shakers                             75
    Guidelines                                                   77

**11 Management development counselling and advisory meetings** 78
Listen for cues and clues 78
Time and place 78
Process consultation 79
Learning from others 81
Managing meetings 82
Guidelines 84

**12 Teamwork from the top please** 86
What is your impact? 86
Management by walking about 86
Top level team development 87
Team management preferences 89
Managerial linkers 90
How team management works 91
As CEO, what will you do? 91
Team meetings 93
Guidelines 94

**13 Management education and the rise of the corporate business
schools** 95
Linking work to development 95
MBA company/university joint ventures 97
Is management education a hoax? 100
Are MBAs worth while? 101
How adults learn 101
What should a manager know? 102
Guidelines 102

**14 The politics of management development** 104
Making plans work 104
Political planning levels 105
Money and management development 106
Political aspects 106
The hard and soft aspects of change 108
International politics and management development 109
A management charter for development 111
Management development in developing countries 112
Management development in Japan 112
Guidelines 113

**15 The success factors of management development** 115
Producing relevant outputs 115
How management development can succeed 116
Guidelines 121

**16 Management development policies and practices** 123
Clear policy and objectives 123
Management development related to business plans 124
Planned, not *ad hoc* solutions 124
Political issues 124
Pay and promotion 125

Management responsibilities     125
Planned job moves     125
Policy issues     126
Guidelines     127

**17   Postscript**     **128**
Ideas for action     128
Summary     128

**Bibliography**     **131**

**Index**     **137**

# Preface

It was, of course, by accident or good luck that I started my own career in the management development profession. When I first went to Bradford University Management Centre, I accepted a job in management education. Little did I realize it would lead me into such an interesting and challenging career.

As a consultant on various management development assignments, I have visited many countries in Europe, the Middle East, South-East Asia, Australasia and, of course, America. I have in the process learned a great deal and, I hope, contributed to the development of others.

As I have recently moved from the university sector to become chief executive in a private enterprise publishing organization, I felt it would be appropriate to summarize some of the key learning points I have gained. As a teacher, consultant and manager I have learned most by involving myself in helping others solve problems and seek opportunities.

Many people have helped me on the way. I thank all my clients, managers, team members and colleagues. You have all shown me what management development is in practice.

For the past nine years I have edited the *Journal of Management Development*, which I founded in 1982. I have learned much from the contributors over the years and have, therefore, included many of these ideas and experiences.

In particular, my thanks go to Rusri Ratnapala, who has word processed this compilation with great skill and patience in a short time. My wife, Colinette, has made it a team effort by editing and producing the final text.

As always, my thanks go to my wife and children for their support. Finally, I thank my parents, Violet and Charles, who gave me a sound upbringing and pointed me in the right direction.

Charles J. Margerison
*Brisbane*
*January 1991*

# About the author

Dr Charles Margerison is the co-designer of Team Management Systems, a new approach to management development.

His involvement in management development includes being Chief Executive of MCB Publications Ltd., a Professor of Management post at the Cranfield School of Management in the UK and later at the University of Queensland, Australia. He has also been involved as a consultant with major organizations such as Mobil Oil, Kodak, Citibank, Burmah, Natwest Bank, Australian Airlines, Aramco and various government agencies.

He is married with four children and lists golf and songwriting among his hobbies.

# Series preface

Training and development are now firmly centre stage in most organizations, if not all. Nothing unusual in that—for some organizations. They have always seen training and development as part of the heart of their businesses—but more and more must see it the same way.

The demographic trends through the nineties will inject into the marketplace severe competition for good people who will need good training. Young people without conventional qualifications, skilled workers in redundant crafts, people out of work, women wishing to return to work—all will require excellent training to fit them to meet the job demands of the 1990s and beyond.

But excellent training does not spring from what we have done well in the past. T&D specialists are in a new ball game. 'Maintenance' training—training to keep up skill levels to do what we have always done—will be less in demand. Rather, organization, work and market change training are now much more important and will remain so for some time. Changing organizations and people is no easy task, requiring special skills and expertise which, sadly, many T&D specialists do not possess.

To work as a 'change' specialist requires us to get to centre stage—to the heart of the company's business. This means we have to ask about future goals and strategies and even be involved in their development, at least as far as T&D policies are concerned.

This demands excellent communication skills, political expertise, negotiating ability, diagnostic skills—indeed, all the skills a good internal consultant requires.

The implications for T&D specialists are considerable. It is not enough merely to be skilled in the basics of training, we must also begin to act like business people and to think in business terms and talk the language of business. We must be able to resource training not just from within but by using the vast array of external resources. We must be able to manage our activities as well as any other manager. We must share in the creation and communication of the company's vision. We must never let the goals of the company out of our sight.

In short, we may have to grow and change with the business. It will be hard. We shall not only have to demonstrate relevance but also value for money and achievement of results. We shall be our own boss, as accountable for results as any other line manager, and we shall have to deal with fewer internal resources.

The challenge is on, as many T&D specialists have demonstrated to me over the past few years. We need to be capable of meeting that challenge. This is why McGraw-Hill Book Company (UK) Limited have planned and launched this major new training series—to help us meet that challenge.

The series covers all aspects of T&D and provides the knowledge base from which we can develop plans to meet the challenge. They are practical books for the professional person. They are a starting point for planning our journey into the twenty-first century.

Use them well. Don't just read them. Highlight key ideas, thoughts, action pointers or whatever, and have a go at doing something with them. Through experimentation we evolve; through stagnation we die.

I know that all the authors in the McGraw-Hill Training Series would want me to wish you good luck. Have a great journey into the twenty-first century.

ROGER BENNETT
*Series Editor*

# About the series editor

Roger Bennett has over twenty years' experience in training, management education, research and consulting. He has long been involved with trainer training and trainer effectiveness. He has carried out research into trainer effectiveness and conducted workshops, seminars and conferences on the subject around the world. He has written extensively on the subject including the book *Improving Trainer Effectiveness*, Gower. His work has taken him all over the world and has involved directors of companies as well as managers and trainers.

Dr Bennett has worked in engineering, several business schools (including the International Management Centre, where he launched the UK's first masters degree in T&D) and has been a board director of two companies. He is the editor of the *Journal of European Industrial Training* and was series editor of the ITD's *Get In There* workbook and video package for the managers of training departments. He now runs his own business called The Management Development Consultancy.

# 1 What is management development?

*The art of governing consists in not letting men grow old in their jobs.*

Napoleon

## Who is going to succeed?

I was in my office one bright summer's day when the telephone rang. The human resources manager of a large engineering firm was at the other end of the line and he asked if I could meet him to discuss some issues about management development. When we met he outlined a fascinating situation. He said he had recently been appointed to a large company with over 10 000 people which had operations in many countries of the world. One of his first tasks was to look at the age profile and the management skills of the staff in order to cope with the challenges of the future. What he found disturbed him and this had led him to telephone me to discuss what could be done.

The organization had established a secure position gaining government contracts based upon its acknowledged engineering expertise. The majority of the managers were technical specialists who had risen through the ranks, based upon experience. They tended to select and promote people in their own image. Therefore, over the years they had established a loyal but rather narrow workforce in terms of expertise and skill. To his horror, my friend found that within the next five years over 30 per cent of the top management would retire and within 10 years well over 70 per cent of the existing management would retire. However, the company had done little to identify and prepare for their replacements.

As he said,

We have a major management development problem. How do we get people who are good engineers to be good managers? We have at the moment over 1,000 managers and we are going to lose 700 of them within the next decade. Equally, our organization is going to lose many of its government contracts and have to become more commercial and compete in a way that it has never done before. We need managers who can develop business rather than just administer it.

He summed the situation up succinctly. However, the particular problem that he posed, is not an unusual one. In many other organizations I have found that they are facing a world of change but they have not developed and prepared their managers to cope with the increasing demand for improvement in the areas of quality, productivity, output, safety, customer service, financial control, new product development, technological innovation and other key aspects, which enable an organization to survive and succeed.

Management development is, today, a top priority for any organization that wants to stay in business. As the emphasis becomes more competitive, with increasing decentralization and people being held accountable on a regular basis for what they are doing, it is essential that we develop managers who can not only produce results themselves, but do so with and through other people. Too often at lower levels, however, I find people being thrown into jobs without adequate preparation.

## Tradesmen and managers

This is most clearly seen in the way in which tradesmen enter into management. I have asked many foremen how they gained their first managerial position. An example from one of them serves to indicate what so often happens.

I had been working on the shop floor in a manufacturing organization for about 12 years. Initially I served my time as an apprentice and then gained experience as a tradesman on various jobs. One day I was approached by a manager and asked if I would be interested in being a foreman. He said I would be on the staff and the wages would be much better. I said yes, but I had no real idea of what I was letting myself in for, or the skills required to do the job. It was a matter of being thrown in at the deep end and learning as I went. I made quite a few mistakes but nevertheless survived.

Another example is that of the research scientist who was asked, at short notice, to take on the management of the company R&D unit. As he said, 'I did not realize what management meant. I had no training for the job and learned by my mistakes.' Unfortunately, examples like this are still very common. It reflects poorly upon middle and senior management that they are not looking ahead and planning the development of people who must take on the leadership roles of the future.

Therefore this book provides a wide range of ideas and practical examples of how to improve management development. They are drawn from various organizations and illustrate the way in which improvements can be made.

## The continuum of management development

Management development, like all aspects of management, requires careful planning. It deals with the whole issue of what managing is about and covers everything from recruitment and selection to self-development, as shown in this structure:

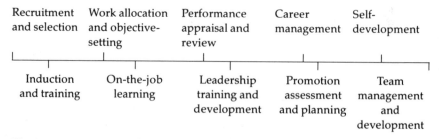

| Recruitment and selection | Work allocation and objective-setting | Performance appraisal and review | Career management | Self-development |
|---|---|---|---|---|
| Induction and training | On-the-job learning | Leadership training and development | Promotion assessment and planning | Team management and development |

These are just some of the key areas, all of which influence the production of products and services at a high standard for customers. The manager's task is to achieve results in a planned, systematic way. This can only be done if those managers feel confident and are trained to do the job across the continuum.

## What is management development?

At the personal level, it is the process by which you and the others gain the skills and abilities to manage yourself and others. Management development is a personal responsibility. Too often managers forget this. They wait for someone else to develop them. They wait for the call to go on the company management development programme. They could indeed wait a long time for today organizations are looking for those who can develop themselves and any company support will only be additional.

At the organization level, management development involves all the issues listed on the continuum—but it is more than just that. Management development is a way of doing business. It is an integral part of management. It is a way of life where challenges are being faced every day and confronted as learning opportunities rather than just a necessity for paying costs and raising revenue. It is where management development is seen as part of the future, rather than simply solving today's problems, that the importance of it becomes visible to all.

In such places you will find a supportive atmosphere conducive to learning. Management development, in such organizations, is the way business is conducted, not something separate to be done when there is no other important work. In short, management development is about how to improve productivity, performance and profit. Management development is a learning process applied to all aspects of work from recruitment and selection, through to delivery of the service or product.

Management development, in my view, is real work. It is not a preparation for work. It is not a substitute for work. It is the real thing if properly organized. Here are a few examples of what I regard as management development for real.

**Example 1**    In a large USA hospital, a group concerned with surgical services meets regularly. Those present are an administrative vice-president, a surgeon. a housekeeper, a supply clerk and nurses from the emergency room and post-operative recovery unit. The group has already been to interview patients, families and doctors. They have also visited the departments that provide services to the surgical group. They have gathered a great deal of information on why breakdowns occur. Their aim is to improve the organization so that the customer gains at the same time as they increase their own and others' job satisfaction. In cutting across such professional levels and involving those who contribute in the diagnosis, they are learning how to manage more effectively. This is management development.

**Example 2**    In an Australian company, managers from different functions are meeting to discuss how to transport materials to their customers. There is a marketing manager, an engineer, an accountant and a personnel manager. They visit the factory and assess the loading processes; they interview transport drivers and go with them on their journeys: they meet the customers and discuss their problems. Once they have all the information, they report to the senior management group to decide what action should be taken. This is management development.

**Example 3**     In a UK company, managers of a major bank are meeting to consider how to improve services. In the group are some customers and bank staff. This is management development.

**Example 4**     In Malaysia, a group of managers are working together to design the bank of the future, in which they will assess what competitors are doing, what the staff want, what the customers need and what will be technically feasible. This is management development.

**Example 5**     In the small South Seas country of Vanuatu, a group of local and expatriate managers meet regularly to study how to improve the local economy and develop their organizations by increasing tourism. They write up their findings and share them with each other. This is management development.

**Example 6**     In a European company a manager meets with each of the staff that report to him and reviews their performance and sets objectives then calls the whole team together to discuss the question: 'How do we as a team improve our management performance?' This is management development.

Such action projects are vital to bring people from different professional groups to learn from each other. It is not, however, just the project that is important. It is the learning process and the fact that all the groups have to show what has been learned by presenting their work to others. Management development is what people do with their learning.

## Managing improvement

Management development, therefore, is an integrated approach to improving individual, team and organizational performance. It is not just a training course. It is not just a good compensation system. It is not simply a good performance review system.

> Management development is a way of managing, not just a system. It involves doing things in a coordinated manner to achieve a result. The management development continuum, therefore, provides a focus against which you can measure performance in your own organization. How well does your organization score on the areas mentioned on the continuum? Allocate a score to each one with 1 being low and 10 being high.

In essence, the management development continuum is the basis of all effective management. You need to look at business objectives and recruit people who can do the job. Once you have employed them, you need to induct and train them effectively so they are competent. You then need to manage them on a day-to-day basis so they are motivated and able to do the job effectively.

In addition, the processes need to be put into timetables so that they are not conducted on an ad hoc basis. For example, there needs to be a regular review of the manpower requirements, and the training and development programme should be worked to a schedule. Likewise, we should have performance reviews carried out according to a plan.

**Structured informality**

At one level, management development involves systems and therefore requires a great degree of discipline, rules and regulations. Management development, however, is also about creative insight. It involves new ways of doing things and providing processes to enable people to come together and share their thinking. It is what I call the structured informality approach.

In this, there is a structure within which people can begin to develop new ways of thinking about how to improve their performance. For example, although there is a performance review system, the way people conduct that must be congruent with their own style and personality. Training and development programmes need to be well timetabled but within the programmes themselves there need to be opportunities for managers to work on real issues and come up with new ideas. Structured informality within the management development approach is, therefore, essential.

**Management development is the key management task**

Overall, though, the continuum points to the need for an integrated approach to thinking about the development of people to achieve business objectives. Look at your own organization and assess where it is strong and weak. That should be the basis for looking at how to improve performance, and the way to do so is to use the management development vehicle as a means to achieve this objective. In doing this, managers will be running two organizations simultaneously.

On the one level, they will be maintaining the operations of the business to produce the products on time, to a schedule and to a level of quality. At the same time they can be developing ways and means of improving the performance. I am of the view that, in the future, the management development approach will be central to every manager's job. They will need to organize time to look at all aspects of the continuum, but particularly to look at how they can improve organizational performance through the various aspects of management development.

# Guidelines

I have recorded the ways in which individual managers and their organizations are both approaching management development. I have drawn together cases, most from my own experience as a consultant, where I have had the opportunity to work with both private and public sector organizations.

The cases reflect many different approaches, for there is no one way to improve managerial performance. I have also dealt with management development in a business-orientated way. It is, after all, in existence to help improve productivity and performance at all levels.

Along the way, I have drawn some lessons and offered guidelines. The test of these is in action, which is the centre of management development. I say this to distinguish it from formal management education, which is but a part of the picture and often not involved with direct action *per se*. How many courses have you attended where you were never given an opportunity to practise what was being preached? Management development is a practical art, founded on experience, guided by technique and occasionally influenced by theory. Management is a disciplined art. The examples, ideas and proposals in this book are drawn from real-life experience and provide guidelines for action.

# 2 Management development as a competitive weapon

*The man who makes no mistakes does not usually make anything.*
William Connor Magee

## Problems as development opportunities

I was playing golf with a senior manager in the building industry. He had recently taken over as marketing manager. We were talking about management practices and he said, 'We have just wasted $50 000 on consultants.' I asked him why. He said that the new division he had taken over had been losing important customers and, prior to his appointment, the previous manager had commissioned a group of consultants to go and interview their major clients.

As he described the situation my friend got quite angry. He said,

We missed a fantastic management development opportunity. We paid $50 000 to a consulting organization to enable them to talk to our customers. We should have paid the $50 000 to our own people and let them conduct the study. In that way, they would really have learned what our customers think of us and what they need.

He went on,

Our own staff would have welcomed the opportunity. It would have helped them develop an understanding of how we can improve our performance. It would also have been cheaper, as it certainly wouldn't have cost us $50 000 to do it. I would like to have seen not only our managers but also other staff members working together in small groups and visiting our customers. Then they could have come back and met with me and other managers to discuss what they had found and what we should do next. In this way we would all have benefited.

This is a classic example of a modern manager who recognizes that management development and the improvement of the organization's competitive position are one and the same thing. The days when we sent people away from work to sit in classrooms and study someone else's organization, through historic cases, are disappearing. My friend was pointing to a trend that will be increasingly prevalent in the next few years. In short, problems are opportunities for management development. In his particular case, he felt that the marketing manager who had commissioned the consultant's report, prior to his arrival, had not only wasted the company's money but wasted a golden opportunity to develop their own people.

## The ICI case

My own work has increasingly involved designing management development programmes around competitive opportunities. In an assignment with the ICI Australian Chemical Company, the Board were concerned that they had too few people in the age range of 28–38 years who could take on senior management positions and asked how they could develop such people. I enquired what were the major business opportunities facing the company over the next three to five years and they identified the importance of converting sound research into commercial processes, the development of new markets, improving customer services and various other assignments.

We therefore identified a number of senior chemists, engineers, accountants and lawyers, as well as people who were already in marketing roles. We chose 15 major projects and allocated them to 15 people who had management potential. Over the next 18 months we worked with them in a practical way one day a fortnight, to enable them to understand the latest skills and methods in finance, operations, marketing, human resources and strategy, while working on the projects outlined by the Board. The result produced tremendous success with major new product developments emerging. In this way, we combined management development with business opportunities. In addition, we provided an opportunity for the participants to write up their work for an action learning MBA degree and over two-thirds succeeded in doing so.

Management development should, therefore, be about action. The action should be tied to the real work of the organization and that is where the focus should be. Improvement should be the name of the game for any management development programme. By giving people real tasks with meaning and purpose to them, you can then have a clear spotlight on what needs to be done. Invariably managers will rise to the challenge of learning and improving. The company, therefore, benefits by enabling its managers to perform more effectively, while simultaneously seizing new opportunities.

## Taking risks

It is not easy to organize a management development programme as a competitive weapon. It will involve risk. No longer can management development be done safely behind classroom walls. It will involve going out and meeting customers and assessing business opportunities. It will involve spending money on real assignments. It will involve senior managers being clear on what they want. Above all, it will involve people meeting to consider what action should be taken as a result.

I have found many organizations who are not prepared to confront the obvious. They are not prepared to allow younger managers to be released upon major strategic opportunities. As a consequence, the younger managers do not develop and feel that their paths are being blocked.

## Managerial support

Where senior managers are prepared to give younger managers real projects such as the launch of new products, the improvement in productivity, the development of better quality and a host of other sharpended, competitive learning projects, progress can be made. Senior management, however, cannot just hand out the projects and walk away from them. They have to be involved throughout, as mentors, as clients, as advisers, to guide and help in the process. In this way, they not only learn themselves, but become committed to taking action on the outcome of the investigations.

In short, if management development is to be successful, it has to be tied to key business strategic objectives. When that happens, all managers can begin to focus the searchlight on how to achieve those objectives by looking anew and developing better processes and practices. In doing so they will develop the people around them. In the company with which I am involved, this has been done on a planned basis. As a result, managers have developed a wider understanding of business by studying areas of work such as distribution, staff induction, marketing processes and costing systems outside of their normal work.

# How to get management development on track

All managers need to have management development at the centre of their agenda. It needs to be the centre of your personal agenda because it is, after all, your career we are talking about. If you do not know how to develop yourself and work with a system that is also supporting those initiatives, then you will be wasting your time.

The result will be that others, who have learned the secrets of management development, will pass you by at a fast rate. Their rewards will be not only a larger salary but more interesting jobs and a challenging and exciting life. Make no mistake, management development is not something to be done on the side. It is central to what your work is about, for if you are not developing, in relative terms, you are going backwards.

Therefore, look at your own organization and consider whether management development is on track. We can first of all identify key factors by which we can discover when it is off track and not working. The usual symptoms are listed below.

## Signs of low effectiveness

1 There is low energy and little direction among senior managers.
2 There is no shared vision of the mission and the objectives of the organization.
3 The emphasis is all on solving today's problems rather than preparing for tomorrow.
4 There is no connection between training and business goals.
5 There is low concern with individual development.
6 There are no systems to review performance and other ways and means of improvement.
7 The culture is more concerned with using people rather than developing them.

These are common syndromes associated with organizations that may be running hard and playing hard but not caring too much that they exhaust the players in the process. Moreover, having exhausted the players they have not implemented any development to bring in the second or third team to take over from the first team.

Another sign of an organization that is off track is that senior managers delegate the management development task to specialists or junior staff. Too many times, in my experience, I have found top managers racing all over the country, jetting about in aeroplanes, doing one deal after another and then finding they do not have the people at the right level to fulfil the obligations they have taken on.

Indeed, it is often worse. I have seen senior managers acquiring companies primarily because of the calibre of the management and then finding that the top performers leave because they object to the new style of management which does not value them and their skills or develop them further. In short, the most valuable asset walks through the door and out of the company into a free market, where he or she can choose an organization that will provide management development opportunities that lead to challenging and exciting work.

If management development is to be taken seriously, the organization should make clear its policy so everyone can see it. Such a statement indicates top management have thought matters through and have provided guidelines to staff.

Figure 2.1 presents the 10-point plan developed by the giant GE Company in the USA in the mid-1970s. It is still relevant today in that it provides broad principles to assess performance in organizations.

---

**THE GE COMPANY**

1 Assuring development of managerial excellence in the company is the chief executive's most important responsibility.
2 Managers at all layers must be similarly responsible and must 'own' the development system(s).
3 Promotion from within for its motivational value will be the rule, not the exception.
4 A key step in planning the development of managers is the manpower review process.
5 Managerial abilities are learned primarily by managing. Other activities are valuable adjuncts.
6 Control of the selection process is essential in order to use openings developmentally.
7 The company can tolerate and needs a wide variety of managerial styles.
8 Several different managerial streams and development planning systems are needed to accommodate the company's size, diversity and decentralization.
9 Occasionally, it may be necessary to distort otherwise sound compensation practice and/or to change organizational structure to achieve developmental results.
10 Staff people must add value in these processes, but their roles are secondary to the managerial roles.

---

*Figure 2.1* *The 10-point plan of the GE Company*

How does your organization compare on the 10 points? In particular, which are the ones that are implemented well and which go by default?

In order to improve performance in your organization, what principles would you add that you feel have already made, or could make, a difference to management development and performance levels?

## A business view

Whenever I am asked to advise on management development, I ask how the plans fit in with the corporate policy and objectives. Too often, in my experience, I have found management development activities, such as educational programmes, being conducted without due regard to what the organization as a whole is trying to achieve.

How many times, for example, have we seen interpersonal skills courses being conducted without any specific reference to the particular areas of the corporate plan, such as improving customer service. Likewise, I am always appalled to see managers and others sent on outward-bound adventure courses with no reference to how it will relate to the corporate objectives of increasing profits. This is not to say these activities will not do these things, but it is unfortunately not clear from the evidence, so far, as to how such a contribution is made.

I have, therefore, come to the view that we need to focus sharply on the way in which management development relates to the corporate plan. Indeed, management development activity should be a way of implementing the corporate plan. I, therefore, look for ways and means by which to bring this about. Management development is the glue that binds policies and plans to action and results.

## Managerial strengths and weaknesses

When consulting on management development, therefore, I start by asking the top management how serious they are about being involved in the management development processes. To do this I have a workshop where I encourage them to identify what they feel are the 'managerial strengths and weaknesses within their organization'.

The results from this simple question are usually most revealing. In the majority of cases the senior management feel that there are more weaknesses than strengths. I often have comments that 'communication is poor', or 'people are not as motivated as they should be'. The important point is to convert the negatives to positives by proposing these as areas that managers should study.

I always get the top management to focus on the key strategic objectives and ask them how far they feel the management development process that exists is satisfactory to cope with the growth they have planned. Again, I often find a major disparity between the plans and the resources. This is the basis for management development action. It is here you can focus on areas for improvements. The skill is in getting the managers to work together in groups, to diagnose the problems and present solutions which can be acted upon.

All of this provides an ideal opportunity to focus on what needs to be done in order to improve performance. By asking top management these questions I get various hypotheses which we can test. For example, if they think communications are poor, then it provides a suitable project to discover in what way and to what extent this is so, and what can be done about it.

**Good business is management development**

In my view, therefore, management development must be driven by the business objectives of the top management. Only then can we begin to identify how many people we need, what we want them to do, what they need to acquire in order to do the job and the various systems that need to be established.

You probably feel this is fairly obvious. In my experience, however, business objectives are often set and pursued without very much discussion about the management development requirements that need to be fulfilled if the objectives are to be achieved. Too often I find top management saying, 'Let us appoint a management development manager to look after these issues.' In this way they feel that they have done their duty and therefore development of staff can be left to a professional.

Management development is, however, the one area of the business that no manager can delegate. It is a personal responsibility, not because it is a good thing to do, but it is essential for survival. If you are not developing your own people, then you are failing in a key aspect of management. You are not helping them to improve their performance and, moreover, you are not developing people to succeed when you move on.

The key test of a senior manager is to what extent there are people who can replace him or her. If you have protected your position by not enabling others to understand your job and the issues that confront you, then you have failed one of the basic tests of management.

**Management development on the business agenda**

In order to make management development succeed, therefore, it is essential that senior managers have that item regularly on their agenda. There should be a quarterly meeting at which progress is reviewed on the total management development plan, inclusive of programmes for development, the promotion prospects of individuals, the selection and development procedures and the way in which the whole process can be improved.

On an individual basis, it is incumbent upon you to set goals for yourself in conjunction with your manager, having the opportunity to extend yourself within the context of the business on a planned basis.

It all sounds easy. In practice it is extremely difficult. Alfred Sloan, when he was the chief executive of General Motors, said that he spent 40 per cent of his time on selection committees and meetings involved in recruiting new staff. When he was asked why he spent so much time in this work, he answered that if mistakes were made by others, then he would have to spend far more time living with the consequences and he preferred to be in at the beginning to resolve matters. It is not only about being in at the selection, but in at the planning and development of people so they can take on wider responsibilities. In this way senior management is doing its job by enabling the organization to succeed.

# Management development and the corporate culture

Mark McCormack, President of the International Management Group (IMG), the organization that negotiates on behalf of the top sports personalities and others in the public eye, has written some 'streetwise' books to pass on his managerial learnings. Each is filled with hard won points that were difficult to see in the heat of the battle. His views on corporate culture are very relevant to management development and I have summarized some of the key points from his book *Success Secrets* (McCormack 1989).

## Recruitment and selection

'Strong culture companies want first rate people.' The hiring process, therefore, is crucial. McCormack says we should tell people how hard it will be, how long the hours will be and then if the applicants are still interested you know they are coming prepared.

I agree with this. In my experience, the most important test—over and above basic intelligence and a modicum of relevant skill in the required area—are the drive, determination and dedication to top performance that people bring to the job. If you can find this out early it will save many hours later.

## Induction and training

Make sure, early in the new person's employment, that the expectations are set correctly. Make the tasks tough. McCormack refers to it as a 'humbling process'. I would not go as far as that. The standard, however, has to be set early and then the people must be trained and developed on a continuing basis to succeed.

## Doing the job

It used to be the tradition that a new employee had to learn the trade from first basics. Much of this approach has gone but at organizations like IBM, all managers have to go through the same field training if they want to progress. Young entrants should be given a wide range of on-the-job experiences.

## Purpose and rewards

People need to know why they are doing a particular task and what they will get for doing it well. When staff understand the importance of work in terms of the customer's quality and time requirements, they can then gear their efforts accordingly. They should be rewarded for achieving the standard and for exceeding it. These rewards should not just be monetary but also promotions and training, plus non-tangible rewards such as appreciation and recognition.

## The culture

McCormack says you should aim to develop a culture where people want to come to work and where customers want to buy. It has to be welcoming but achievement orientated. People like being part of success. Management development, therefore, should encourage and help people at all levels to be successful. I agree that is the key part of the manager's job.

# Guidelines

Management development should be at the sharp end of the business, helping to reduce costs, increase sales and improve productivity. It should be a process whereby managers and other staff develop through the process of doing and learning at the same time.

Everything in business can be studied with profit in order to improve it. In the act of doing so—providing the emphasis is placed on learning and development in an orderly way—individuals and teams can develop. Every aspect of business, therefore, should be a subject for study, whether it be the operations management and cost effectiveness of the filing system through to the creation of policy and its implementation.

Management development is the core of any business. Ignore it and you close down the future of the business. Management development is more than the recruitment and training of the new managers; it is the process by which the company is managed in order to secure the future.

What does your company need to do to improve its management development performance?

# 3 Improving and reviewing performance

*Whoever acquires knowledge and does not practice it resembles he who ploughs his land and leaves it unsown.*

James Ross

## Describing performance accurately

'The problem with performance appraisal is that most people think it is a good idea but few people know how to do it well,' said a colleague. I believe he is right and it is important that we all learn how to review performance and give feedback.

The answer lies in asking people to review their own performance. I have therefore encouraged all managers with whom I work to set up performance reviews, whereby the subordinate is given a structure within which to write down what he, or she, has done and how it has been done. This written assessment, completed by the individual, then forms the basis of a discussion between the boss and the subordinate.

In such discussions, the objective of the manager, initially, is to ask subordinates to provide examples and illustrations of where they think they have done well and where they have done less well. The objective is not to make judgements but to try to help improve performance.

## The performance appraisal case

I was asked by a large division of an engineering company to do a management review of their performance appraisal system. They had an agreement with their unions that required feedback on the total process. From the 4,000 staff, 10 per cent were included in the review which was conducted by a questionnaire.

It was a conventional top–down system where the manager assessed the staff. The staff felt the appraisal system was sound, that the paperwork was clear, that managers took it seriously and sufficient time was allocated to it. All looked fine until the second part of the review when I asked performance expectation questions, such as, 'As a result of the appraisal interviews, do you believe you will work harder, less hard or the same?'

Other questions asked whether their relationship with the manager had improved, or whether they felt their career prospects had improved. The answers were mainly 'No'! In short, the staff thought the system was alright but nothing would change. The problem was, the staff felt little or no responsibility. It was the manager who wrote the appraisal. They only had to sign if they agreed with it. Little of real value, therefore, came of it.

I recommended the system be turned upside down. First, the staff would write their own performance appraisal. This should then be the basis of a discussion with their manager, who could add any points after hearing the views expressed. This enables the manager to become a consultant to his or her staff rather than a judge.

## Positive feedback

Most of us like to know whether we are doing a good job. However, this needs to be phrased in a positive rather than a negative way. If someone tells you that 'You are poor at writing reports' or 'Not very good at making presentations', this in itself is not particularly helpful. It tells you what you are not doing. It does not tell you, however, what you could be doing and how to achieve it.

Feedback, therefore, has to start with a diagnosis with the person who wants to learn. Second, it needs to be discussed with someone who is willing to talk through specific examples and illustrations of performance and give guidance on how that can be improved. This needs to be followed up by guidance, advice and help on a regular basis, so that the person can begin to see that he or she is improving.

## Specific feedback

It is important though that personal feedback is given in a helpful way. Where the manager feels that the subordinate is not making an accurate assessment, he or she should say so, but should do it in a way that provides specific examples and illustrations rather than generalized statements. For example, if a subordinate says, 'I have written good reports' but the manager feels this is not so, then it is appropriate for the superior to say, 'I feel that the reports you produced could be improved by having them in on time and by having more facts in them rather than just opinions.' Now this is specific feedback and indicates it is designed to improve rather than just criticize.

All of this will improve their confidence level. The result will be improved performance and higher energy levels. In this way, managers can have a real impact upon the way in which people do their job and, as a consequence, will benefit themselves as it will make their job easier to do.

## Action steps

1 Identify key areas for performance review based on agreed objectives already established.
2 Ask your subordinate to write a review of his or her performance and send it to you.
3 Meet, undisturbed, to discuss the written assessment.
4 Ask questions to understand, not judge.
5 After you have heard his or her views then add your own.
6 After the appraisal review set the objectives with your subordinate for the next period.

## Team building— improving teamwork

A manager is only as good as his or her team. The reason you are appointed manager is because there is simply too much work for you to do completely by yourself. The effective manager, therefore, spends a lot of time developing a team of reliable people who can work well together.

Most managers are not in a position where they can go out and pick the people they want to have working with them. They inherit a team and have to develop ways and means of getting support and cooperation. Let us look at the ways in which this can be done and at the same time foster the management development of the individuals and the group as a whole.

The first thing that a new manager can do is to act as a consultant rather than as a manager. You are in a position to ask a lot of interesting questions, both individually and collectively. If you want to encourage an open environment where the team shares with each other information and ideas, then it is useful to start as you mean to go on.

When Sallyanne Atkinson became the Mayor of Brisbane, one of Australia's largest cities with a population of over a million people, she acknowledged that her largest previous management job was that of mother to her five children. She therefore came to her job asking questions rather than giving directions. She visited the engineers' department and the highways' department and asked them why they did things the way they did. She said, 'When they couldn't tell me, or gave answers that didn't seem sensible, that was the area for improving teamwork and I asked the manager to do so.'

**Reviewing team development** One way to improve teamwork is to call a team meeting and say you are interested in finding out how they feel the team works together.

It is then useful to put two questions—these are:

1 What does the team do well?
2 What does the team do less than well?

If you have a large team it may be useful to divide them up into two groups for a discussion of about 20 to 30 minutes, while they consider the points among themselves. However, if it is a small team, then it is useful if they just discuss the points with you. The important thing, whether it is done in groups or as one whole team, is that the points are written up on a flip chart or whiteboard so that everyone can see.

**Personal involvement** It is vital that you personally sit in on the discussion and hear what people have to say. If it is a small group you may wish to act as the scribe and put the key points up on the board. Alternatively, if there are a number of groups, you should probably sit with each for a period of time and hear the discussions. It is important to show that you are personally interested and not aloof from the process.

When the groups report back and tell you what they feel they do well and what they do badly, do not criticize or deny any of the points. Accept them in the spirit in which they were offered. Your task is to get the groups to discuss what they are going to do with each of the points.

**Strengths first** First of all, start with the things they do well. Ask them for examples and the way in which the team has performed in the areas they mentioned. This is often very reinforcing. It is usually the first time the team has been asked to talk such matters over and, in doing so, they can communicate to each other things that perhaps have not been said, and thereby raise morale.

The key point of the discussion, however, is to ask them what they can do to improve the situation even though they have done well in the areas mentioned. You should still look for areas of improvement. Try to get them to identify what can be done and how it can be achieved. This can then provide a basis upon which further discussions can be held at the next meeting.

**Examples and illustrations**

The next area is perhaps more tricky. People usually do not like discussing things they have done badly. However, if you set the right environment and encourage people to consider areas of their teamwork that are not going well, then you can begin to get major improvements. If, therefore, people say that communication is bad, ask them for examples.

At that point you can then begin to think positively about how they could improve matters. When anyone offers an idea, record it and have it discussed. If there is debate, encourage people to give it a trial, or at least to have the person who suggested it go away and produce more information at the next meeting as to how to make it work. The object is to encourage people to communicate and participate.

**Team improvement**

In this way you will have started the process of team building. The team will in fact have done it for you providing you encourage them. Your role in team building should be to help them achieve what they know can be achieved. Therefore, it is vital that you follow up within three to four weeks and have a meeting to see what they have actually done. The proposals from this meeting can then be incorporated into the way in which you wish to manage the group.

Team building, therefore, starts on the first day you join a new group. It is then a continuous process of getting them to discuss with you areas in which improvements can be made. It requires confidence and the willingness to risk hearing information that may not always be favourable.

That is, however, an integral part of what managing is about. The job involves raising the energy levels of people to improve things. The best way towards doing this is to ask them to assess for themselves what needs to be done and then, with your permission, guidance and ability, obtain resources in order to improve the situation.

# The team appraisal workshop

A key aspect of improving management performance is to design a process to enable people to consider issues of importance. I will outline an example and show its place in management development.

I was invited by a group of colleagues with whom I worked to help them assess how they, as individuals and as a team, were performing. This case study provides an example of the processes that may be of help to you in your work.

Prior to the workshop, there was considerable apprehension among a number of the team members. Some were publicly sceptical of the whole exercise. Others thought it would be a useful thing to do but were not sure whether it would have any real value. There were others, noticeably the chief executive, who were very enthusiastic and regarded it as the only way in which an open and positive discussion could take place about how the team could improve its overall performance. It was felt, therefore, this needed to start with a discussion on how individuals saw their own work performance as a basis for discussing the wider team effort.

The workshop was, therefore, designed to last at least half a day and up to a whole day if required. It had a number of stages, which were based upon the principles of self-appraisal identified above.

**The agreement and the system**

Initially, there was a thorough discussion among all team members to ascertain the willingness of people to participate. Despite the scepticism, it was agreed that a team appraisal workshop would be held and everyone would contribute. At this meeting, a number of guidelines and procedures were set out and agreed to. These involved the circulation prior to the meeting of an appraisal sheet, whereby each person wrote down his or her own appraisal, which was then to be sent to the team leader and me. The next point that we agreed was the structure of the workshop.

I decided to set up a very straightforward and simple self-appraisal form based on a number of open-ended questions. The original document, together with the questions, are outlined below and this provided the basis for the data that people were asked to produce prior to the meeting. These data were then circulated to the chief executive, who coordinated the main points. Each person was also invited to send his or her self-appraisal documents to other members of the team. In the event, most members of the team did so. The self-appraisal document is presented in Figure 3.1 and the questions that people were asked to respond to are given in Figure 3.2, overleaf.

---

**THE SELF-APPRAISAL DOCUMENT**

**Each year we shall review our individual performance in our roles so as to:**

1  **identify the key achievements;**
2  **identify areas that need further personal effort;**
3  **develop personal performance plans and any training or resources required to achieve the plans;**
4  **enable the Group chief executive to understand the views of colleagues.**

---

*Figure 3.1*

**The workshop**

The workshop was held off site. A country house was selected as the venue, so there would be no interruptions of telephones or customers or any administrative problems. We also decided to hold the meeting at the weekend so that people did not feel that other work was being neglected.

---

**PEER PERFORMANCE REVIEW**

1 During the past year the following are the *key outputs* I have managed:

........................................................................................................................................

2 During the same period the areas I feel I did *not achieve the outputs
 necessary* were:

........................................................................................................................................

3 The areas I think I need to *improve* my personal effort are as follows:

........................................................................................................................................

4 The issues I wish to raise for discussion at my review are as follows:

........................................................................................................................................

5 Can you describe what the company means for you now and over the
 next two or three years?

........................................................................................................................................

---

*Figure 3.2*

The guidelines for the meeting were again simple and straightforward. I
introduced the workshop by re-capitulating the objectives that had been
agreed at our first meeting. These were that we should appraise each
other's performance with a view to improving our effectiveness both as
individuals and as a team.

I, therefore, initiated the debate by saying that each person would be
the chairman of his or her own appraisal, and that, as chairman, he or
she was to manage the meeting in a way that provided and obtained
information relevant to the work that person did. To do this, each person was asked to summarize his or her own appraisal document within
five or ten minutes. Thereafter, the person would chair the ensuing discussion.

At any point in the meeting the person, as chairman, could conclude the
proceedings by saying to the other colleagues that it was now time to
discuss the work of someone else. However, a time limit was also
placed upon the discussion of any individual's performance so that
everyone was given a fair hearing. Initially the time period set was half
an hour, but in certain cases this was extended to one hour.

My own role was to act as chairman to the chairmen. Initially, therefore,
I set proceedings going with the first appraisal. It involved one of the
team members, who, prior to the meeting, many people felt had not
performed as well as perhaps they had expected. Somewhat to everyone's surprise, this person said what others had been saying privately.
He acknowledged that he had not given as much time as he should to
certain projects. He recognized that there had been areas in which he
should have put more effort. He acknowledged that his own work had
not helped other colleagues at particular times.

This initial appraisal in many ways set the tone for what was to follow. It provided the atmosphere of open debate that is essential in meetings of this kind. People in the meeting, therefore, began to explore with this team member how his performance could be improved and the way in which they could help. In fact, other points of criticism were also made but, at the same time, credit was given for specific work that had been done.

**The discussions**   Initially there was a tendency to hold back. However, some of the more sceptical members who had doubted the value of the team appraisal workshop prior to the event, were the most hard-hitting when it came to dealing with specific issues. It was they who asked the pointed questions, such as what a particular member was going to do to improve his or her performance in a specific area. Equally, all members were active in indicating where other members had made it difficult for them to do their job properly and asked what they felt could be done for the future as well as making specific suggestions.

The debate was lively. As the coordinator I found very little need to intervene, although from time to time made some process comments. These were more to facilitate the positive side of the discussion rather than have a particular issue thrashed into the ground. In many ways the most difficult part of the job was ensuring that people kept to their time.

The agreement had been that each individual should have an opportunity to discuss his or her work and clearly the person who was going to come last in the gathering was going to meet rather a tired group. It was important also to maintain the momentum and, therefore, I asked on a number of occasions for people to press on with the overall review rather than become too involved in specific detailed issues, which could be dealt with at length outside the particular meeting.

At the end of the meeting there was a general feeling that it had been extremely worth while. Most people felt tired. However, it was generally considered that a number of important things, which had not previously been said publicly, had been brought to the attention of individuals and the feedback had been taken and discussed. The critical question was whether it would have any real effect upon subsequent behaviour.

What was clear was that there was now a determination to be more open about the way in which people confronted colleagues, and certainly this has been evident in meetings since that time. It has also facilitated decisions regarding promotions and pay. Indeed, since the team appraisal meeting, this has had particular importance in that very critical decisions have had to be made regarding the rewards made to certain members due to changes in business conditions. These decisions were made, again publicly, and willingly accepted by the members concerned.

**The value of team appraisal**   Team appraisal is not a substitute for the conventional individual performance appraisal; it is complementary to it. The strength of team appraisal is that it produces an opportunity for people to talk out, at a colleague level, the issues which previously have only been debated between the manager and the subordinate or privately in corridors when people have been 'talking behind other people's backs'.

The team appraisal, if done well, can act as a major reinforcement to a person's own plans and commitments to do better. Having talked through one's ideas, aspirations and ambitions, there is then a keenness to achieve what has been discussed. There is a lot of evidence to show that where a person does discuss matters with colleagues, there is less back-sliding and more commitment. Therefore, as an approach to motivation, team appraisal (see Figure 3.3) has much to commend it.

---

**TEAM APPRAISAL SUMMARY**

- Each team member writes his or her own appraisal based upon agreed open-ended questions.
- Each person forwards his or her appraisal to the team leader, who holds a performance review meeting with that person.
- At this meeting the appraisee talks through the issues raised, and the team leader then can add comments to the appraisal document as a result of the discussion.
- This meeting should cover past, present and future performance for the next period under review.
- The individual performance appraisal is the prelude to the team appraisal where each member is chairman of his or her own team review.
- Each member of the team receives everyone else's initial personal self-appraisal (*not* the one containing managerial comments).
- The focus of the discussion is on how individual team members have helped or hindered others in achieving team objectives and action that can be taken to improve team work.
- The team leader is accountable for writing up the outcomes of the team appraisal and managing the team and its members along the guidelines agreed.

---

**Figure 3.3**   *Team appraisal summary*

It is also a key way in which a manager can show his, or her, commitment to an open managerial style. While the issues of pay and promotion were not on the agenda in the meeting, the issue of performance certainly was. I believe it is important to separate these factors. I consider that the issues of pay and promotion should, within a hierarchical structure, still be the managerial prerogative in discussion with the subordinate. However, performance I believe is a colleague prerogative and requires discussion with all those who are influenced by one's performance.

## Guidelines

Team appraisal is a long way from form-filling and ritual annual discussions. It brings alive the real value of the appraisal process. No longer is it a secret meeting whereby a manager states his or her opinions to a subordinate. It becomes, instead, a basis for an open debate about the way in which a group of people are going to work together.

Given the increasing number of people from different professions who have to work together in the modern organization and their high level of educational attainment, I believe the team appraisal workshop will become an integral part of the managerial style and approach, adopted by many organizations. It will be no different from the normal annual or quarterly financial audit and review procedures.

It is certainly equally important and the work that we have done so far illustrates the value it can have. It is an integral part of effective management development.

# 4 Management development and added value

*Some people have greatness thrust upon them. Very few have excellence thrust upon them. They achieve it.*

John Gardner

## What is the value of management development?

I am firmly convinced that management development must prove itself sooner rather than later, by adding value. Too often it has failed to achieve this. We have spent a lot of time providing information, giving lectures, running training programmes, taking part in outward-bound adventure exercises, teaching case studies, running simulations, and a host of other well-intentioned activities, which, however, are unlikely to add value in the short term and, maybe, never.

The reason is simple. All the methods avoid action. They do not deal with the real world. They are in essence preparatory for doing something, rather than dealing with the main priority of adding value to a service or a product.

I therefore ask anyone who wants to start a management development programme, 'Why are you doing it?' In particular I ask, 'What are the economic issues that you are trying to improve? Are you trying to reduce costs, or increase sales or improve productivity?' If so, these are very clear ways of adding value. We can then begin to discuss the specific tasks that need to be worked upon to do that and gear our management development activities around them. In this sense we are focusing upon the outputs rather than the inputs.

## Outputs as a priority

If management development has had a weakness over the last 25 years, it is that we have focused too much on inputs rather than outputs. We have been too preoccupied with giving people skills that they *might* need, rather than specific tools they *do* need in order to improve the added value of their work.

The only way to solve this is to ask people what tasks they are working on, or are going to work on, and then design the management development activities around those tasks. Some people will see this as rather a limited way to approach the development of managers. They will say that managers need a broad-based education such as you get on an MBA programme.

## Practical applications

However, in my experience there is nothing to stop managers learning the wider aspects of their profession by starting from a particular project or task in which they are trying to improve the added value. Only recently, I was working with a group of managers from various organizations who were all concerned with ways in which they could improve productivity in their respective jobs. Once we had established the tasks, we were then able to talk about the concepts and skills they could use for a whole range of functions such as marketing, finance, operations, human resource management and strategy.

Indeed the conversation developed to look at key issues and the psychological aspects of work and how these affected projects, together with an analysis of organizational sociology and the structure of the organizations. Beyond this we talked about the way in which the national economy and the international business affected their own work and looked at various trends and developments that were occurring.

## Establishing a purpose

In short we were able to move outwards from the specific to the general. In so doing, however, we were focusing our attention and studying in a highly relevant way. We had a purpose. The managers knew why they were gathering information skills. They were, moreover, able to go back and apply this knowledge in terms of improving their own performance and tasks within their organizations.

Let us, therefore, always consider why we are engaged in management development. The key task is to add value. It is not just an individual development exercise. This can be done by people in their own time. The function of management development is to enable a person to manage other people more effectively and to achieve better results in a more efficient and effective way.

## Executive education in major corporations

In an important USA study, Albert Vicere and Virginia Freeman (1990) investigated how over 150 major companies conducted executive education and development programmes. The most prominent executive development techniques that were identified are shown in Table 4.1.

**Table 4.1**  *Executive development techniques*

| Technique | Response frequency (%) |
| --- | --- |
| Job rotation | 72 |
| External executive programme | 48 |
| In-company development programmes | 47 |
| Participation in task forces and projects | 32 |
| On-the-job training | 28 |
| Coaching/mentoring | 26 |
| Performance feedback | 6 |
| Teaching/consulting with other employees | 1 |

I find it surprising that such practical techniques as putting a marketing person on a production task force or a personnel person on a product distribution project are so little used. Clearly these USA organizations have quite a way to go in making their executive education more sharp ended.

Indeed, from my own experience, the last item listed in the table is one of the most powerful development techniques. I have found accountants widening their grasp of marketing and marketing people beginning to understand accounting when they have to help each other understand their own area of specialism—particularly when it involves a joint project.

Let us, therefore, keep our eye on the priorities and ask on each occasion how far the management development activity is adding value. If it is not doing this, we are probably not aiming at the right targets. We are probably wasting people's time. We are probably using valuable resources in the wrong way. If we focus on adding value and ask everyone who is involved in management development how they will achieve such ends, we shall then have a *raison d'être* to gather what we do.

## Small business for management development

There is no better training ground to develop managers than to give them an opportunity to run the business. Clearly, a young manager cannot be placed in charge of a large company. However, he or she can be given a part of the business to run as a profit or loss enterprise. This is superb training for any manager.

Increasingly, organizations are recognizing the need to decentralize and with it comes more opportunities for managers to run a business within a business. When I asked one senior manager what had been the biggest learning experience in his managerial life, he said, 'When I was given an opportunity to run a small business which I could put my arms around and say, I'm responsible for that.'

### The motorway warehouse case

A classic example of this kind of thinking is possible where companies are prepared to structure their operations into venture companies. One organization with whom I worked did this in a very spectacular way. They encouraged ideas from young managers in their late 20s and early 30s on how to improve profits. One particular manager put forward a proposition that the company's products, instead of being sold through retail outlets, should be sold in warehouses at the end of motorways.

Instead of rejecting this rather outrageous idea, the directors voted to give him over a million pounds to set the business up. It is now an established operation and very successful. In the process, the manager learned a tremendous amount about the total operations of a business.

It is this all-round management development that we must encourage. Managers, in order to grasp the totality, must have experience of what it means to produce as well as to market, and how to finance the business, as well as manage the staff. In the process, they will begin to think strategically and learn the key aspect of management.

## Business responsibility

Some organizations are already well structured for this. Retail organizations notably give managers opportunities in their late 20s and early 30s to run shops. They have to buy in their stock, merchandise it, relate with customers, manage staff and ultimately produce a profit. It is an exceptional training ground for any budding manager involved in running a shop.

If you want to develop managers who have an all-round view of a business, structure it so that there is an opportunity for profit and loss experience. It is not too difficult, providing you are prepared to have a small head office and act as a 'banker' to the chief executives of the many small businesses. Some organizations, like hotels and indeed banks, are so structured to ensure many managerial opportunities where a person can put their arms around the organizational unit and say, 'that's my profit centre'.

To do this, we need to think markets, and we can then begin to structure the business so that we create units in which managers can interface with customers and, at the end of every week, can assess what was spent and what the business earned. This kind of structure will sharpen managerial thinking and performance and be the centre-point for management development.

Therefore, I favour and argue for more customer-focused business units. When a company is restructuring, I ask: Who will benefit? If it is the customer who benefits by faster, more efficient and better quality service, then that is usually good for management development at all levels. The McDonald hamburger phenomenon is cited many times as an example of leading management practice. Its frontline managers, albeit franchisees, see the customers every day.

## The playing field

Managers will only develop if they practise. Lesson number one, therefore, is to provide the playing field for as many as possible to practise (Figure 4.1). It will provide many coordination problems higher up the managerial structure, but that is the price of training 'hands-on' managers who understand the market.

One of my friends left school at the age of 16 and started work in a local factory that made shower screens. He quickly learned the manufacturing processes and asked to go on to the building sites to gain orders. He established good relationships with the builders and generated many sales orders. When the factory manager retired, my friend, who was then 23, was asked to succeed him. 'I had a team of 40 people depending on me. I knew how to build and how to sell. I had to learn quickly how to manage the staff and make sure we had enough money to pay the bills. I kept close to the staff and close to the customers. They taught me a great deal and we did well.'

He did so well that, within five years, the parent company—an international conglomerate—promoted him to national marketing manager. 'Without the early all-round experience, I would not have had the confidence to take on such a large job.'

In the large bureaucratic organizations, however, where there is a high degree of centralization, it is often difficult for managers to get hands-on experience of running a total operation. For example, you may have spent years in an accounting function or managing an engineering operation. You know a great deal about that particular aspect of management but you have never had to deal face-to-face with the hard realities of buying and selling and paying wages every week.

Buying and selling concentrates the mind and brings home the realities of the difference between cash flow and profit. It highlights the importance of recruiting and selecting good people and training them. Above all, it develops you because you are involved on a day-to-day basis in thinking through how to improve not only your own performance but the performance of the business for which you are responsible.

---

### DO YOU WANT TO PLAY THE MANAGEMENT GAME?

1  **The big move is on to decentralize large organizations.**

2  **This is good news if you want to rise to the challenge.**

3  **It will mean greater opportunity to have a real say in the business, and in particular, the chance to manage a business unit on commercial lines.**

4  **To do this you will need to be skilled in managing many aspects of the business beyond your original specialism.**

5  **You will need to develop yourself to speak the languages of marketing, operations, finance, human resources, information systems and strategy.**

6  **You will need the skills to find out what is required, analyse the information, identify options and implement decisions.**

7  **A key to it all will be your ability to develop an effective working team who will have the motivation and determination to see it through.**

8  **Your job is to be the key linker, the conductor of the orchestra, helping them solve the problems as a group, rather than just as a collection of individuals. See your group as a total business that has to make a return on the assets (your team and resources) and proceed to become efficient and effective against agreed standards.**

9  **You will be measured on your performance against set objectives and you will have to assess others accordingly and decide how to improve people's performance or make the hard decision.**

10  **It won't be easy, but it will be exciting. Do you want to do it? If so, start making it known you want to be part of the game. It's called management development.**

---

*Figure 4.1  The management development playing field*

## Guidelines

I therefore advise organizations, wherever possible, to structure themselves so that they give people opportunities to run a small business before they ask them to take on the management of a large business. In this way people become 'street wise'. They learn to find out what works.

They get close to the customer. They begin to realize the key factors between success and failure.

If you wish to develop as a manager, therefore, seek an opportunity to run a small business where you can be a general manager even though you may only have 5, 10 or 20 people reporting to you. You can then see the total picture and get a feel for what it is like to understand the dynamics of business life.

1 Identify the key aspects of your job that add value.
2 Consider options and ideas for improving the added value—what can you do?
3 Set a plan for implementing the ideas—with whom must you work and what must you do?
4 What outputs are you aiming for?
5 How will you review your performance?

These are the issues that will concentrate your mind on the management development that you and your colleagues need to succeed.

# 5 What do managers want from management development?

*The people who get on in this world are the people who get up and look for the circumstances they want and if they cannot find them, make them.*

George Bernard Shaw

**Develop terms of reference**

A large organization employing 7 000 people asked me to advise them on developing a policy and plan for executive development. I asked them to identify the terms of reference, and at a two-hour meeting with the chief executive he outlined a number of key points.

- He wanted people within the organization to have opportunities to grow and develop and to move to senior posts.
- He wanted at least 70 to 80 per cent of all appointments to come from within the organization.
- He wanted a participative approach to management where people had the opportunity to put forward their ideas and make the maximum contribution.
- He believed in self-development and felt that everyone should have the opportunity to improve (regardless of whether or not they were in line for promotion).
- He felt that people could learn best from tackling challenging work assignments and that this should be an integral part of the way in which managers managed others.
- He believed that values were important and that people should have an opportunity to think through the way in which they translated their philosophies and ideas into day-to-day practice.
- He believed it was important that managers cooperated across departmental lines and, wherever possible, tried to gain experience outside their own technical area by interchanging from time to time with other managers.

In short, he had a very clear set of principles, against which he wanted policies and programmes to be framed. He said that he therefore wanted a steering committee to take these ideas and to work out how best to implement them.

**Steering committees should steer**

When I met the steering committee they felt they knew what was required and should therefore come up with a policy and programme. I counselled them against this saying that we had only the chief executive's perception of what executive development should be about. I said, 'These are important guidelines but they are not necessarily what other people in the organization feel are important. All those who are going to be involved in the executive development process should be consulted.'

Some members of the steering committee felt this would take too much time and would be complicated. There were lots of arguments about how difficult it was to get people away from their jobs. One member of the committee said, 'There are already too many meetings here and people won't thank us for involving them in more meetings to discuss this.' Another member said that the issues were pretty obvious already and they had been appointed as representatives of management to come up with ways and means of moving things forward. Another member suggested that a questionnaire be sent by me to all the senior managers involved as this would get the required answers.

However, I said that it was nevertheless important to hear the views of other people personally. The chairman of the committee said the best way, therefore, would be for me to attend the weekly staff meetings held by the line managers. This, he said, would disrupt procedure to the very minimum and enable me to hear what people thought. Again I counselled against this, as I could see that executive development would be the tenth item on the weekly agenda and I would get five minutes at the end of a meeting dealing with financial, operational and other day-to-day matters.

The CEO had said he wanted more participation; therefore, the process of diagnosis should be participative. For this reason I held my ground and insisted on separate off-site meetings with the managers. It was just as important for each manager to hear the views and learn the needs of the others as it was for the steering committee.

After much discussion it was agreed that three workshops should be assigned where people could come on a day that was convenient to them. I allocated two hours to each of these meetings and invitations were sent out. In all, there were 45 top managers in this organization and, eventually, 36 of them attended the various meetings.

**Develop meaningful questions**

Three questions were put to them, which they were asked to discuss in groups:

1 What in your experience are the strengths and weaknesses of management in this organization?
2 What do you personally want from an executive development programme?
3 What do you believe should be the key principles contained within a policy on executive development?

We had about 12 people at each of the meetings. Much to the surprise of the steering committee, the meetings were not only well attended but the participants had strong views on what the current situation was and what should be done in the future. They not only gave examples but indicated what they felt should be done. As one manager said, 'We don't want more formal courses where we are given lectures on what to do. What we want is an opportunity to improve performance and learn in a practical way.'

Another manager said, 'The most important thing is to help us develop a network where we can begin to cooperate and communicate more effectively with each other.' Another said, 'I've learnt most by being on different kinds of projects, which have helped me move outside my own technical area and this is what we should be doing.'

**Managers should set their own agenda**

They, therefore, began to set their own agenda of what they wanted to do and how they wanted to do it. They also began to indicate clear issues on policy governing recruitment and selection and the basis for reviewing performance and promoting people. The discussions provided the essence of what executive development should be.

I then gathered this information and took it to the steering committee who were able to develop a policy and programme that were then fed back to all the managers. This became the basis for gaining agreement on how to proceed. When the policy and programme were launched there was a high degree of commitment because the people who were going to run the policy and the programme had been personally involved. This is the way in which managers should be in charge of their own destiny, as far as executive development is concerned.

If you really want to ensure that management development is a success, start by involving the managers themselves and discussing their own needs and how they can best be satisfied. Don't be surprised if they are initially critical of the organization and what has gone before. Use this to develop ideas on what can be done to improve the situation. In this way managers will own the management development agenda and make sure the service that is provided is relevant to their needs. They will also be committed to supporting the programmes and processes that emerge.

Increasingly, managers are looking for development opportunities as an integral part of the job. Whereas they are keen to be paid well, they also

---

**IBM—EMPHASIS ON DEVELOPMENT**

Thomas Watson Sr, the founder of IBM, believed that the annual investment in education, training and internal communication should increase at a rate that was greater than the company's rate of growth.

In his book, *The IBM Way*, Buck Rodgers (1987) indicated that Thomas Watson believed that between 40 and 50 per cent of top management time should be spent in educating and motivating its people. With over 40 000 employees and 1 500 managers, that commits a lot of time to management development. In IBM a first-line manager receives 80 hours of classroom training during his or her first year on the job. In addition, much training is founded on the recognition that a great deal of management skill requires effective communication and people management. Of course, there are opportunities for senior managers to attend programmes outside the company and meet with other executives.

While IBM is recognized for its educational programmes, Rodgers however emphasizes that the real test is on the job. As he says, 'Productive people need challenging assignments. It is vital for them to go home at night feeling that they did something worth while.'

now look for work that enables them to extend themselves and develop new skills and competencies. Management development is, therefore, increasingly regarded as part of the compensation package. When a new manager is deciding whether or not to join an organization, he or she will look for the development opportunities.

It is, therefore, vital that management development be seen as an integral part of work rather than something that is added on. It should, moreover, be seen as something for which managers are looking as part of the total package of rewards they get from a company. Whereas money can buy food in the shops, experience is the passport and working capital for personal development and success.

Any executive who is worth his or her salt will want to go beyond where they are. This means creating opportunities, both within the job and outside, to enable them to continue learning and developing. In that way they are being rewarded at the high personal level of self-development rather than just having cash in hand. Reward in this sense is an integral part of personal growth.

# Assumptions, prejudices and hypotheses

I was asked by the Board of Directors of a congolomerate to give a talk on what management development meant. I refused, politely, but offered to meet with them to discuss what management development meant to them in their company.

When we met, I asked them what they felt were the strengths and weaknesses of management in their organization. They identified important points. However, I suggested these points were assumptions, prejudices and hypotheses, which should be tested.

The Board agreed to appoint three project groups to test their views. These groups were the start of a wide-ranging management development programme. The whole approach was based upon managers identifying areas they felt needed change, and appointing managers from various functions and groups to work together to discover ways of improvement.

As a result, a high level of energy was applied to a range of issues such as 'How do we export more?', 'How do we train supervisors?'. All this came from involving managers in discussions on what management development meant for them.

As the managing director said during the sessions, 'We may, or may not, earn a dollar from all this but it will sure develop our managers to do so in the future.'

# Why managers leave

I have often heard managers say that they left a company because they felt that they were no longer learning or making progress. They had become bored. Their income at a psychic level started to decline, and they therefore looked for new challenges.

It is vital, therefore, in your organization to question how far the company is providing challenge to its executives. If the company is growing, expanding, taking on new markets and launching new products, then it is probable that you will be able to reward people through job challenge. Equally, however you must provide people with the opportunity to develop the confidence and skills to take on those challenges.

Where the company is in decline and is losing market share or is having to reduce its costs in order to stay in business, then it will be much more difficult to provide such a challenge.

In future, management development will increasingly be an issue which managers will consider high on their list of items when establishing a contract with a company. This is not only for newcomers but for existing employees who, on an annual basis, will be renewing their contract with you. If they do not feel they are getting an income of development to match the income in their pocket, then it is likely they will feel that the latter will decline as they grow older.

As a test, therefore, talk to some of your managers and find out what they feel about the management development opportunities in the organization. To what extent do they look for opportunities to develop themselves? You will probably find high interest in this and it is incumbent, therefore, on the company to look at ways of improving what they often say is their most important asset—their people.

## What makes a manager?

A study that gained a great deal of publicity and a large number of followers was *The Competent Manager*, by Richard Boyatzis (1982). He involved over 2 000 managers, who were in 41 different managerial roles in 12 different organizations.

He identified, from this work, the following managerial competencies which, he claimed, were related to effective managerial performance. These were: an efficiency orientation, pro-activity, diagnostic use of concepts, concern with impact, self-confidence, use of oral presentation, and conceptualization. For managers at middle and executive levels, he also emphasized the use of socialized power, managing group processes, perceptual objectivity and self-control.

As a result, many people have gone out to measure competencies and to train people in them. They provide a useful checklist. Certainly we should move to an approach based on job demands and the organization environment for developing competent people to handle these issues. What is now important is that potential and actual managers have the opportunity to practise their skills in a situation where they can receive feedback and improve. It is the management development implications that are the vital ingredient, rather than trying to divine whether or not someone has or has not the competencies.

Other major studies, such as those by Stewart (1967) and Kotter (1988), provide valuable insights into the characteristics and requirements for managers. It is difficult, if not impossible, to tell in advance who will succeed and who will not. Picking the winners in the managerial game is a difficult exercise, as any recruiter will tell you. It is better to bet, as one manager said, 'on the devils you know than the ones you don't'. That is why management development is so important.

**Management development preferences**

There is no one best way to develop as a manager. Each manager has a preferred way of doing things and a preferred way of learning. It is influenced by such things as whether you are more extrovert or introvert; more practical or creative; more analytical or belief orientated; more structured or flexible in your approach. Dick McCann and I (Margerison and McCann 1990) have explored these issues in the context of our work on people's career journeys. People's work preferences influence the ways they wish to proceed and the work they do.

However, the higher you go in management, the more is there a need to have what staff at the Shell Company call 'a helicopter view'. This means understanding various functions of management and how they relate. It also means learning and using a range of managerial languages. This we call developing linking skills, and it is the ability to become a good linker that will determine how successful you are in management.

# Approaches to management development

My colleague Alan Mumford has advanced three interesting and useful types of management development (1988), and I have reproduced them in Figure 5.1 overleaf as they provide a good checklist for managers. Which of the approaches fits with your learning and work preferences?

# Guidelines

In developing a management development programme, ask the managers what they want. They may not know how best to deliver it but they will usually know what will help them improve their performance.

Do not be put off by those who suggest it is too difficult to gather people's views rather than regret the lack of consultation at a later point when the managers complain about not being consulted.

To ensure cooperation, involve managers in your assessment of needs and get them to diagnose their needs. Keep it all simple, however. You do not need a major academic study lasting months, but a short, sharp set of meetings. The word will quickly get round that you are serious; but beware, do not ask managers their views unless you *are* serious and intend to take relevant action on what they say.

---

### Type 1   Informal managerial—accidental processes

*Characteristics:*

> Occur within managerial activities
> Explicit intention is task performance
> No clear development objectives
> Unstructured in development terms
> Not planned in advance
> Owned by managers

*Development consequences:*

> Learning is real, direct, unconscious, insufficient.

### Type 2   Integrated managerial—opportunistic processes

*Characteristics:*

> Occur within managerial activities
> Explicit intention both task performance and development
> Clear development objectives
> Structured for development by boss and subordinate
> Planned beforehand or reviewed subsequently as learning
> experiences
> Owned by managers

*Development consequences:*

> Learning is real, direct conscious, more substantial.

### Type 3   Formal management development—planned processes

*Characteristics:*

> Often away from normal managerial activities
> Explicit intention is development
> Clear development objectives
> Structured by development by developers
> Planned beforehand and reviewed subsequently as learning
> experiences
> Owned more by developers than managers

*Development consequences:*

> Learning may be real (through a job) or detached (through a
> course) and is more likely to be conscious.

---

*Figure 5.1*   *Model of types of management development*

# 6 How to learn from action

*I have learned more from my mistakes than
from my successes.*

Humphrey Davis

I have been convinced now for some time, that the best way to develop
managers is to give them challenging jobs but with a support system
that helps them learn. Being thrown in the deep end is a dangerous way
to learn to swim, unless you have someone who can help you. Of all
the approaches I have seen, action learning is by far and away the most
effective, although difficult.

## Learning from action

The fundamental ideas were originally propounded by Reg Revans
(1982). He developed the ideas from his scientific work, where he and
his colleagues would meet to share their problems and difficulties. In
talking through the issues, they began to help each other and this led
him to the view that the principles (Figure 6.1) could be applied to
management development.

When he became the Director of Education for the National Coal Board
in the UK, he encouraged colliery managers to visit each other's mines
and learn from each other. After the visits, he brought them together to
share and compare what they had gained and found that they had
learned a great deal. One manager who was excellent at cost control
was able to share his methods with others and someone else, who was
very good at safety management, could reciprocate.

He took his ideas on action learning into other organizations, most
notably the hospitals. He found that by bringing together doctors,
administrators and nurses to work on common problems and share
their ideas, patient care improved. In particular, the hospitals in which
he worked were able to show that patients were in hospital for a shorter
period. He then applied his ideas to industry, but most noticeably with
the larger manufacturing companies. His considerable work in Belgium
led to the formation of an inter-company consortium.

I have implemented the action learning ideas proposed by Reg Revans,
and they work. They particularly work in adding value. The reason they
work is that they deal with the reality of the work situation. Managers
bring along issues of economic significance and begin to talk through
how they can improve performance. This is, however, not just a pooling
of ignorance as some people have suggested. It is an opportunity for
managers not only to share their own experience, but to learn from others
who have special expertise.

**KEY PRINCIPLES OF ACTION LEARNING**

1 Management development must be based on real work projects.

2 Those projects must be owned and defined by senior managers as having a significant impact on the future success of the enterprise.

3 Managers must aim to make a real return on the cost of the investment.

4 Managers must work together in groups and learn from each other, crossing functional and departmental boundaries.

5 Managers who undertake the projects must be charged with the following through the analysis to gain real action and change.

6 Managers must study both the content (programmed knowledge) and the process (questions and methods) of change.

7 Managers must publicly commit themselves to action and publicly report on outcomes achieved.

*Figure 6.1  Revans' principles for management development*

**The MFS Chemical Company case**

I was invited to work at a chemical refinery that was having problems in reducing the number of accidents. I asked the senior managers to identify the key safety areas. They all identified projects where they would like to see improvements. These included an audit of fire prevention procedures, an improvement of the apprentices' safety record, the distribution of dangerous goods, the safe loading of chemicals and many others.

We then brought together managers and supervisors from the plant and spent three days discussing how they could study these areas of safety with a view to making improvements. We asked them to work in groups and the senior manager nominating the action learning project had to brief them on the task. Thereafter, we counselled and consulted with them but left them to get on with the job of diagnosing the problems and developing solutions. The results in all the areas, by the admission of senior management, went far beyond expectations.

The particular case of transporting toxic chemicals from the factory to the customer was interesting. A group was formed which included an accountant, an engineer, a computer manager and a marketing executive. The marketing man initially objected saying that the transport of toxic products was not his problem. He said his job was to plan the marketing strategy and work with the salespeople. Reluctantly, he nevertheless joined the group. We showed him and the group how to go about conducting an action learning assignment and over a period of three months the group studied what happened to the chemicals as they moved from the factory to the customer.

At the end of three months, at the report phase, the marketing manager stood up and said that he had been wrong. After conducting the study, he had come to the conclusion it was not the people in the factory who were causing most of the accidents, nor even the people who transported the toxic chemicals. The major problem was with the farmers who were the customers: they were handling the chemical in a nonprescribed way. He concluded, 'We must spend more time educating our customers.'

On the same programme a group of managers were asked to look at the reasons why apprentices had more accidents than tradesmen. On the surface it looked a simple task but all previous efforts to reduce accidents among apprentices had failed. We, therefore, asked the managers to form an action learning group and encouraged them to do the obvious—talk to the apprentices.

To their surprise, no one had brought all the apprentices together before. When they did, they found that the apprentices not only knew why the accidents were happening but also had many ideas on how to stop them. When one of the executives asked why this information had not come forward before, one of the apprentices said, 'No one ever asked us.' It was in this way that the apprentices were encouraged to form a group and start learning how to improve their own performance.

**Other action learning achievements**

We have used the same approach on such issues as productivity, cost reduction, sales improvement, quality improvement and such motivational issues as absenteeism. Once people have the opportunity to study their own work environment and seek ways of improvement, they become motivated to do so providing they know they have the permission to implement what they have discovered. In the process they learn an enormous amount.

The International Management Centres under the innovative leadership of Gordon Wills (1986) have established the only business school dedicated to improving performance by action learning. It now operates in 18 countries with over 1 000 associates, many doing MBA-level degree work. All study is based on real projects and taking action. Associates have to study marketing, finance, operations, human behaviour and other subjects but, most of all, must apply them to action. Increasingly, major organizations are supporting this radical work-based approach to development. Companies like ICI, Dupont, Seagrams, Grand Metropolitan, Cummins Engineering and others are launching their own in-company MBA-level programmes tutored by IMC staff.

I have been involved personally in the action learning MBA programme as well as the non-qualification work and have been genuinely impressed by the action and learning achieved by the managers. As a result, I have been pleased to be involved as a vice-president of the organization and a tutor on many programmes.

I have found that managers learn a considerable amount

- about themselves
- about their job
- about team members and, most of all,
- about how to improve things and make changes.

**Action learning at GEC and elsewhere**

In their book, Casey and Pearce (1977) provide excellent examples and illustrations of the work they and their colleagues did at the GEC in the UK. The managing director, Lord Weinstock, had by chance seen Reg Revans expounding his views on television and invited him to work

*Table 6.1 Comparisons of learning methods*

| Traditional learning | Action learning |
| --- | --- |
| Individual based | Group based |
| Knowledge emphasis | Skills emphasis |
| Input orientated | Output orientated |
| Classroom based | Work based |
| Passive | Active |
| Memory tested | Competence tested |
| Focus on past | Focus on present and future |
| Standard cases | Real cases |
| One way | Interactive |
| Teacher led | Student led |

with managers in his organization. The results of this action learning effort had a major impact on management development in the company as well as resolving specific problems.

A most interesting review of action learning projects is also provided in Mike Pedler's book *Action Learning in Practice* (1983). Again the examples show the power of action learning as a vehicle for change in many situations, including community groups as well as industrial and commercial situations.

A publication that directly sets out to show the relationship of how action learning can positively influence management development was edited by Alan Mumford (1989) and produced as a special edition to honour the work of Reg Revans. The evidence on a personal, group and organizational level is impressive and indicates that action learning demands more serious attention from managers and management development professionals than it has received so far.

It is therefore a surprise to me that action learning has not had a greater impact on industry. People often discuss it, but do little about it. The ultimate test of action learning is effective action. Something must happen, otherwise we shall not learn.

In action learning we are reversing the normal process whereby we assume that we learn something and then take action upon it. Instead, action learning requires that we put forward a project, a problem or an issue and go into the world to tackle it and, in so doing, learn key managerial skills.

# Illustrations of action learning

There are many examples of organizations that have used action learning to improve performance. These are a few I know, or with which I have been associated:

1 Human resources groups from a consortium of organizations met in the UK, over a period, to share and compare action projects and learn with and from each other.
2 State Government branch directors worked in trios visiting each other's branches to advise and comment on how to improve each other's organization and develop their own skills.

3 ACI, an Australian company employing over 20 000, adopted action learning to provide managers with cross-company experience of operations and issues working in sets of mixed disciplines and functions with four people to a set.
4 A postal service organization trained new mailroom managers by a three-month action learning programme rather than the traditional 10 weeks off-the-job classroom approach.
5 A manufacturing company which had to reduce costs by 10 per cent did it by involving the managers in an action learning set and saved $250 000 in three months.

I have written a short managerial guide to action learning (Margerison 1989) which summarizes the major points that should be considered if you intend to implement the process in your organization.

## The basis of managerial learning

Action, however, by itself may not be the answer to managerial tuition. We must support the action by other activities. Kolb (1984), and later Honey and Mumford (1986), have shown these needs to be a continuous cycle for which they have developed measures involving the following activities:

• experience
• reviewing the experience
• concluding from what has been learned
• planning the next steps, which will involve further experience.

This is a useful checklist and can be used to improve your learning process.

Another way we can consider the learning process is to think of it in terms of a game. I have used golf as an example. Here you can learn by:

• having a round of golf (*action*)
• discussing the round with others (*reflection*)
• taking a lesson from a professional (*tuition*)
• reading about the game (*consideration*)
• watching other players (*observation*)
• going onto the practice ground (*experimentation*)
• developing new thoughts (*planning*).

All of these and more can be applied in management. The important thing is to have a systematic approach and take managerial learning seriously. I believe one of the best methods is to write down what you do and, alongside, put notes on what you will do to improve your performance. You then have a reference check on the action you take.

I believe there are three key areas, as shown in Figure 6.2 which relate to

• doing
• knowing
• learning.

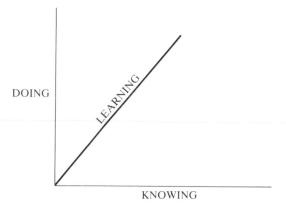

**Figure 6.2**　*The three main areas of management*

Your task is to maximize these areas. You can do this by taking a planned approach and ask

- What do I need to know and how can I find out?
- What do I need to do and what schedule have I for achieving it?
- What shall I learn as a result and how can I use this to improve performance?

Look at Figure 6.2 and give yourself a score out of 10 on each of the arms. In which areas do you need to put more effort?

## How managers learn from experience

Management development involves the ability to learn from experience and put that learning into practice. This comment, from a general manager, illustrates the point:

I never really knew what overheads were until I had responsibility for them. I had read all the books and I knew intellectually what an overhead was, but it was all theoretical. The day I became general manager, and looked at our business from that perspective, I suddenly realized the influence and significance of overheads. I had to manage them. I had to make sure they did not get out of control. This was a major learning experience for me and it shaped not only my management thinking but my management development. I began to see the business as a totality. Now I try to encourage my staff to do this and have regular reviews when I get managers to look at not just their areas but the central overhead as well. If they are going to be general managers they have got to really understand it and make the right decisions.

This was one manager's view of what to him was a crucial learning point in his own management development. I have asked other managers what they have found to be the vital aspect, and a summary of the various responses is an interesting indication of what has to be learned if you are to succeed as a manager. I have put the comments which come from various interviews in quotes and given each an alphabetical reference.

A 'Understanding the real difference between cash and profit was an eye opener for me. I had read about it but the first time we almost ran out of cash and I had to pay the bills. It made me think a lot.'

B 'Managing people whose work I did not understand taught me a lot. I was trained as a chemist, but when I was made manager of Research and Development, I had physicists, engineers, biologists and other professional groups reporting to me. I realized then that management involved a lot more than technical knowledge.'

C 'Pricing was a subject I tended to take for granted. When I had to set prices I agonized over the decisions. What if the customers refused to accept the increases? It was then I began to take an interest in the wider aspects of consumer behaviour and I gained a better view of what we were doing.'

D 'I have always listened to the one liners that more experienced managers have told me about, such as "the smarter we work the easier it is" but it was only when I became a senior manager I realized I had to think out the smarter ways. I now have "let's get smart" meetings.'

E 'Distribution was always someone else's problem. My job was to make the product. I improved my management skills the day I moved downstream and realized nothing has been accomplished till the customer gets the product.'

F 'On most management courses the lecturers invariably say people are important. I found that out when we expanded too quickly and we didn't have enough good people. I learnt that developing people beyond their existing jobs as soon as possible is the way to keep me out of trouble.'

These vignettes tell us how some managers learn. Usually it is through the school of hard knocks and the ability to avoid the problem a second time by taking corrective action. You can no doubt think of similar experiences in your own career. The important point, however, is to capture those learning experiences in such a way that managers can get together and share what they have discovered. Too often the lessons learned by one manager are not passed on because there is no forum in the company to do so. If experience is one of the best teachers, we need to provide internal workshops so that people can share their learning.

# Reflecting on experience

My colleague, Alan Mumford (1985a), has helped managers learn a great deal from experience. It is a resource often underused and ignored. Most managers are surprised at what they know when they have a chance to express themselves in a planned way. It was Alan Mumford who introduced me to the learning log book—a bit like a diary, only covering key management issues. He has also designed various development events based on what managers have done, are doing and plan to do. The key on each occasion is the sharing of experience.

In these workshops comments such as those above are made. Instead of being ignored, they are put centre stage as that is the cue for a learning opportunity. We can all learn from others if we take the chance and in return are willing to share what we have gleaned on the road of experience.

## Guidelines

There are many examples that are a testament to the success of action learning. The real problem is getting managers to have the confidence to try it. For every organization that has done so, I can tell of many more who found reasons not to take the risk of allowing people the freedom to challenge the status quo and develop in the process.

Here is what you can do if you want to take the risk of improving performance and learning at the same time:

1 Identify areas where there are problems or opportunities.
2 Call together those who are involved and ask for specific projects to deal with the issue.
3 Get people who do not normally work together to share their skills and experiences on the issue.
4 Ensure they meet regularly and also report back to colleagues at a presentation meeting every month.
5 After three months, conduct a review on how to further improve performance.

## Questions at the end of each day

The following are useful checklist questions:

1 What did I learn?
2 How did I learn it?
3 What action shall I now take?
4 How shall I assess the improvement that occurs?
5 With whom shall I share the learning?

These five single questions are powerful searchlights on the road towards management development. One way to stay on track is to keep a diary and put down your thoughts on these issues daily, or weekly, or monthly. You will then see what you are learning and the impact it is having.

More important, encourage your team to do so and get together to share your learning points. Do likewise with your colleagues. You will be surprised how much you will gain and the appreciation others will have for your contribution.

Management development does not have to be expensive, but it does involve taking some risks.

# 7 How to make career choices

*Far more crucial than what we know or do not know is that we do not want to know.*

Eric Hoffer

It is important, when we are developing others, to look at the experience gained by senior managers. I have had the opportunity to obtain the views of over 250 managers in the UK and another 700 managers in America, all of whom have reached the chief executive position. I asked them what they felt were the important factors in enabling them to reach the level of chief executive.

It is clear that chief executives attribute their success primarily to their own personal drive and aptitudes, together with practical involvement in situations where they are able to gain experience and learn by 'doing'. Indeed, they rate the contribution made by formal training relatively low down the list. It is also interesting to see that sound technical training rated only 14th on the list of factors. The 10 major issues that the managers in the UK and the USA felt to be important are listed in Table 7.1.

*Table 7.1 The 10 most important career factors*

| Factors | USA | UK |
|---|---|---|
| 1 A need to achieve results | 1 | 2 |
| 2 An ability to work easily with a wide variety of people | 2 | 1 |
| 3 Job challenge | 3 | * |
| 4 Willingness to take risks | 4 | 7 |
| 5 Earlier overall responsibility for important tasks | 5 | 2 |
| 6 A breadth of experience in many functions prior to age 35 | 6 | 5 |
| 7 A desire to seek new opportunities | 7 | 11 |
| 8 Leadership experience early in career | 8 | 4 |
| 9 An ability to develop more ideas than other colleagues | 9 | 8 |
| 10 An ability to change managerial style to suit the needs of the situation. | 10 | 10 |

* Not included at the time of the UK surveys.

## The key factors

It is clear that the need to achieve results and the ability to work easily with a wide range of people are seen by the USA and UK managers to be the two key factors. These come before such technical issues as having a knowledge of finance, or marketing, or industrial relations, or operations. They come before the understanding of strategic planning or the tangible items such as knowledge of company products and processes.

The top five factors that chief executives value are personal drive combined with interpersonal skills, a challenging job and willingness to take risks and have responsibility. After those come the breadth of experience in many functions, plus a desire to take new opportunities and have early leadership experience.

We can conclude, therefore—looking at other people's experience—by saying that if you want to develop as a manager, you need to take responsibility for your own development. Above all, you have to set challenging targets and develop the ability to get work done through others. This has been said many times, but it does seem that chief executives recognize these to be the prime skills and act on them.

## Personal experiences

I interviewed many of the chief executives and they all had interesting experiences that had shaped their own approach to management. They could all remember vividly the day they took their first managerial command and, at the time, felt it was a daunting task. What struck me, as I interviewed these managers, was their views on how they solved the problems. It was not a one-man show. They quickly learned to work with a team and coordinate them.

They were not scared to ask others to do complex jobs but they gave intellectual and moral support. They spent much time planning with their team members, and then let them have responsibility for action.

Many admitted they made mistakes. As many executives said, 'That is the only way you really learn.' The secret, however, as one mentioned, 'is always to assess the risk you are taking so that, if it goes wrong, it will not ruin you or the organization'.

In all the conversations it was clear that the CEOs, while recognizing the support from others, put the emphasis upon self-achievement. They set themselves goals and worked in a disciplined way to achieve them. Above all, they took responsibility for their own management development.

## Personal follow up

What should you do if you wish to move in this direction? The first act is very much in your own hands. No one is stopping you setting objectives and managerial goals: it is a question of getting out of bed in the morning, identifying what has to be done and setting yourself a disciplined plan to achieve results.

Do not, however, forget the factor that goes with this hard task-orientated approach. It is the softer factor of working with and through other people. It is a question of involving them, and getting them to participate and put forward their ideas on how best to improve performance. You need to be skilled in designing meetings to get the best ideas, and skilled in working with people to implement those ideas.

Therefore, look at your own career and check whether you are setting high achievement standards. Check the extent to which you work well with others. Consider whether your job offers challenge. Also look carefully and see what risks you are taking and ensure that you are prepared to take overall responsibility for important tasks.

Perhaps even more important questions are: 'To what extent are you doing this for others?' and 'What example are you setting?' Identify your own subordinates and assess each of them on the criteria listed in Table 7.1. How well do they compare if measured out of 10 on each of the factors that the chief executives identified?

If they do not rate very highly, perhaps you should discuss with them what they should do to improve. Equally, if they are doing well you should give them feedback and encourage them in their aspirations to become better managers.

We can all learn much from experience, particularly the experience of those who have already succeeded in reaching high managerial positions.

**Other developments**  My colleague, Andrew Kakabadse, with whom I worked on the American CEO study, also did further work on the careers of police officers (1988) and female managers. He found similar patterns and concerns. He also developed an interesting approach by looking at management from a political point of view (1983) and assessed the part played by politics in day-to-day work situations.

**What job do you want?**  The management development process is of course about making choices, whether they be personal or corporate. We have to decide whether or not we wish to chase high-level managerial jobs. Until recently, it was difficult in most large organizations to gain high reward and status unless you moved into managerial positions. Now it is being increasingly recognized that there needs to be a management development scheme of sufficient width to take account of other options whereby, for example, technical people can remain as specialists.

While working with a number of companies looking at these issues, I have been able to identify four major options that people can choose as part of their development process. These are reflected in the career model roles shown in Figure 7.1, overleaf.

# Making career choices— options

**Specialists**  Some people can make their best contribution as specialists and we need to have structures that enable them to pursue their careers and make the best use of their abilities. They usually have narrow experience and a low interest in managing others. They can, however, be world beaters in their field. In the group there may, for example, be a top sur-

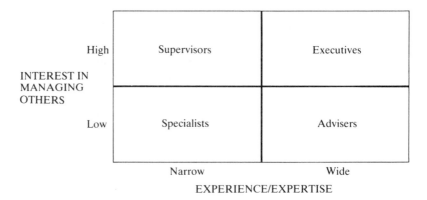

**Figure 7.1**  *Career role models*

geon or a world-renowned chemist. It is vitally important that, as part of our overall approach to management development, we provide opportunities for such people to do their specialist work without feeling that they have to assume administrative activities. This is an integral part of management development, even though they will not become managers in the traditional sense.

**Advisers**  Increasingly, the modern organization is dependent upon people who have excellent advisory skills. Such people usually have a wide competence and experience, but, like the specialist, a low interest in managing others. They are nevertheless essential, moving across the organization to facilitate improvements and provide the support necessary—whether it be giving financial advice, legal advice, training advice or the many other forms of consultative support—to ensure that work is done.

**Supervisors**  Supervisors are key people in ensuring that the work gets done. Their role has long been recognized from a training perspective, but perhaps not so much in terms of the management development process. Such people usually have a high interest and capacity to manage others, but often work in a relatively narrow area of experience. The foreman or forewoman is a classic case, where he or she may have very good managerial skills but is limited in terms of future promotion by his or her technical knowledge and background. It is important, however, that they be developed in the wider sense, in order to make the most of their potential as supervisors.

**Executives**  This is the traditional area in which management development has been seen to have its major focus. Such people usually have a wide area of understanding and competence in the business and also a considerable interest and ability in managing others.

In order to get this breadth of experience, it is important that they go through what I have called the tough approach to learning on-the-job and not be left in the one position for too long a period, if they have potential. Indeed, it is likely that many executives will have started as specialists and then moved to supervisory and/or advisory positions before progressing into the executive role. I believe that this is a very important aspect of management development, during which time they can be exposed to many of the work functions mentioned above.

---

**PETER DRUCKER'S VIEWS**

'Development is always self-development . . . the responsibility rests with the individual, his abilities and efforts.' This is the view of Peter Drucker, probably the most influential single management consultant of our time.

Drucker's views on management education reflect his own experience. He decided at an early age he did not want to lead or manage others. His autobiography (Drucker 1982), which is well worth reading as a self-development text, is called *The Adventures of a Bystander*. He recounts how he was at the front of a parade carrying the banner when he decided he wanted to communicate and report, rather than be an executive leader.

He nevertheless has had a major influence on those who do lead. In particular, his opinions on management education and development have begun to challenge the conventional wisdom. Drucker has questioned the value of long periods in a classroom away from the laboratory of experience. He argues that there is a need for a closer involvement of on-the-job and off-the-job learning.

*The Effective Executive* (Drucker 1988), is a valuable guide to anyone who wants to improve their performance and a reference book on management development priorities.

His advice to managers, in order to improve effectiveness, is:

1 Record your time and avoid time waste.
2 Know what you contribute and assume responsibility for improving it.
3 Make your strengths productive and work on the things you do well.
4 Concentrate and establish priorities.
5 Make effective decisions based on the good ideas, backed up, as far as possible, by solid facts.

These give a good basis for any manager, providing the principles are converted into relevant action.

---

## Early job experiences

There is some evidence to indicate that the initial jobs a person has in management are of considerable influence on later performance. Manuel London (1984), while at AT&T Communications Corporation, did some interesting work on how to develop new managers. He built on the work that indicates that early socialization has an important impact and conditions people to performance levels.

He devised ten 'commandments' for developing new managers which I have reproduced here, as I believe they are vital to the induction of any manager, particularly new ones.

## Ten commandments of development

1 Have an accurate and thorough assessment of skills and abilities.
2 Give individuals major responsibility for development so that the programme reflects individual strengths and weaknesses, preferences and goals, etc.

3  Set target job(s) and time frame(s).
4  Provide challenging job assignments as early as possible.
5  Assign individuals to effective role models who can provide enabling resources.
6  Provide objective job performance feedback.
7  Ensure accuracy and realism of expectations.
8  Expose individuals to a variety of functional areas within the departments.
9  Ensure a high level of commitment and involvement on the part of top management and participants.
10 Allow periodic evaluation and redirection of career plans.

To what extent did your own induction score highly on these points? What will you do to improve the induction of new staff?

## Assessing action levels

In order for us to assess our own and other people's abilities and preferences we need to understand the key options before us. The role performance model, Figure 7.2, provides a simple checklist against which we can begin to see the options. This can be used to assess people in all the roles mentioned. In all jobs we are being tested and in order to move to the next level we need to perform. *En route*, however, we may find that we are rated initially as people who do have problems and then move into a situation where we are assessed as having either potential, or become a possible for advancement.

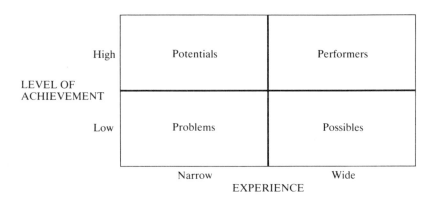

*Figure 7.2   Role performance model*

What do we mean by the terms in Figure 7.2?

• *Performers* are those people who have a high need for achievement and produce results based upon a wide background of experience and expertise within particular roles.

• *Potentials* are people who have shown a high need and level of achievement but so far do not have the range of experience or expertise to do a wide range of work in their professional area. These people clearly need development opportunities.

- *Possibles* by contrast are people who have been exposed to a wide range of experience and have expertise but have yet to show commensurate levels of achievement in a particular role. Clearly, this involves an analysis of how they are being managed and a discussion with them through the appraisal process of their own preferences.

- *Problems* are people who, within particular roles, have shown little achievement and have a low level of expertise and experience. This may, however, only relate to a particular role and in some other job they may well be performers. It may also relate to the early stages of taking on a new job when they are experiencing difficulties and need guidance and support.

This model provides a quick guideline against which you can assess not only your own position but that of other colleagues. It provokes the question of what can be done to help people move into the performer category. Rather than just leave it to chance, specific activities should be set out and agreed, on a regular basis, in order that people can learn and develop into performers.

## Management education and development

In my experience, most management education programmes favour the performers and the potentials. It is difficult to design programmes that generate high achievement levels; but it is possible, however, providing the individuals are involved in group projects where they are carried along by group peer pressure. This may last for the length of the programme but will it have any effect thereafter? This depends on whether line managers use the same principles to ensure that low achievers do not slip backwards.

I have been involved in many short, sharp executive education programmes that are high on knowledge input but do little, if anything, to cope with experience or achievement levels. The result is the proverbial 'seven-day wonder'. After a week, the educational injection wears off and everyone reverts to normal behaviour patterns. It is vital, therefore, to ensure that executive programmes are an extension of work and that work is a planned integration of the educational programmes.

## Guidelines

So, what choices will you make? Do you wish to be a supervisor, a specialist, an adviser, or an executive? Once you decide, develop a plan for achieving your objectives. Make it a schedule based on outputs you will achieve within given time periods and allocate the costs and benefits. In this way, you will move from the problem area through the possible and potential areas to the performer area.

Therefore, to develop, you need to have your own plan of campaign. It is no use leaving it to others. Consider, therefore, what you want to achieve and set yourself

- knowledge objectives
- skill objectives
- experience objectives
- work achievement objectives.

These should be done at least annually and reviewed quarterly. If you plan your own development as well as any manager plans the company's budgets or sales, then you will be on the right track.

# 8 Colleagues, managers, customers and competitors— keys to development

*Dost thou love life? Then do not squander time, for that's the stuff life is made of.*
Benjamin Franklin

## Ways we can learn from colleagues

We can all learn a great deal from others. We all have different ways of managing. It is those differences that provide a tremendous opportunity for us all to learn how to improve. In this chapter, we shall look at some examples of how you can learn from people with whom you work.

It always astounds me, however, that so little is done by managers to learn from other colleagues. Naturally, we all take up ideas on a casual, informal basis. There is, however, relatively little done in an organized way to enable colleagues to learn from each other.

## The retail company case

I have taken these ideas and used them in a wide variety of settings. A large retail chain store approached me and asked how they could develop their managers' competencies to take a wider view of the job. Initially, they wanted me to run a short training programme in the conventional way with lectures, videos and group discussion. I discussed the pros and cons with them and found that their real objective was to improve not only managerial knowledge, but cooperation between the retail store managers.

It then became clear that there was an unwritten rule that no store manager could visit another manager's store because this was seen as trespassing on someone else's territory. There was a suggestion that this may be regarded as spying and trying to discover the weaknesses of another manager's operation. The managers, therefore, tended, to avoided each other's stores.

They were, therefore, not learning from each other. I indicated to the chief executive that there was a great opportunity here for interstore visits. He was somewhat hesitant and thought the store managers would not be very keen. I persuaded him that it would be useful to discuss this at our next meeting with them. When I put the suggestion forward, the store managers, much to the surprise of the chief executive, agreed.

The results were most encouraging. The store managers began to identify areas in which a colleague's performance was better than their own. Some had better layouts, others had better staff teamwork, others had better cost control. When we met to discuss the findings, there was considerable interest in what had been learned. There were many indications of how they had put the learning into practice to improve their own store and their own performance.

**The government department trios case**

In a similar case I took the idea of learning with and from each other to a government organization. There, a number of senior managers ran branches involving anything between 20 and 300 people. I persuaded the managers to join me on a two-day workshop. We discussed teamwork and how they could work together, in trios, to help each other's performance.

We created five trios and considered ways and means in which they could assist each other to improve managerial performance. They arranged, between themselves, interbranch visits in which I, and a number of colleagues, acted as consultants to the groups. We met with them on two or three occasions after they had conducted a visit. Each person in the trio invited his two colleagues to help assess ways of improvement. Following this, we had a one-day review, at which all the trios had to report on what they had done and what they had achieved. There was a high level of enthusiasm and energy. They all had tales to tell of what they had learned from their colleagues and what they were doing, or going to do, in order to put such ideas to work in their own branches.

At the same time there was a steering committee, of the top management group, to whom the managers reported. At our meeting with the committee members they indicated very strong enthusiasm for the programme from their colleagues but they themselves felt left out. They saw the changes that were occurring. As one of them said, 'I notice a much greater openness and willingness to share among the branch managers, which wasn't there before.' They felt, however, they also needed to be involved and it was agreed that the principles should be applied at the top level as well as at the branch.

The programme continued over a period of three months and, as a result, a considerable change in culture occurred. Instead of people being protective and defensive about their departments, they became more open and willing to share and learn from others. The great benefit came from the better relationships that were established between branch managers.

In addition, individual managers indicated greater confidence. As one of them said, 'Visiting other colleagues' branches has been an eye opener to me. I realize now, how well we are doing. I've been able to contribute to others what we do, as well as learn from them.'

**The airline case**

Finally, as another example of how to encourage sharing and learning with and from others, let us consider a case involving airline pilots. I had assumed, before accepting this job, that the captain, first officer and flight engineers would form a close knit group, who would regularly learn with and from each other. However, I was wrong. Most airline crews, having finished the job, go home.

When we were approached by the airlines to improve teamwork, I therefore asked how often the captains, first officers and flight engineers met to discuss how to improve teamwork. The answer was, 'They never do unless they are having an overnight stopover on a flight.'

We therefore organized a three-day workshop as the basis for getting people together to discuss how they could work with each other to improve performance. Yet again, we saw that the captains, first officers and flight engineers, despite initial scepticism, found the whole thing most beneficial. As one of them said to us late at night at the bar, 'This programme is great because it provides, for the first time, an opportunity to talk over with each other how we manage the process of flying, rather than just being on another technical course.'

If you really want to learn how to manage, therefore, set up a process with your colleagues to do so. Do not leave it to chance; it will not happen by accident.

## Manage the experiences

Learning from others must be planned in such a way that there is co-operation and goodwill. Ensure, therefore, that you get a group of people that can be together for two or three days, and discuss how they will do it. Ensure that they will work in duos, trios or quartets to some specific purpose. They can decide what project to tackle, how to do it, when to do it and where to do it, but they must report back to everyone else. Make sure this happens within about six weeks of the first meeting. Along the way, give them guidance, thought, and whatever help you can by way of reading materials and resources. However, let them do the job, and let them find out from each other what can be done.

Once you have had a mid-programme review, ask them then to concentrate on implementing the ideas that have been discovered. Ask them to help each other put the ideas into practice. Then bring them back again after another six weeks and ask them to report, preferably in front of their senior managers, on what they have done, how they have done it and what results they have achieved. In the process you will find they not only learn but will actually improve their performance.

You also can do it if you want, but it has to be done in an organized way rather than just hoping that someone will teach you something.

## Learning areas

What is it, therefore, that you should seek to learn from other managers? The first thing is that they are probably doing a job at a different level from yours. If you have aspirations to move up, you need to know what issues they are confronting and how they are dealing with them. (See Figure 8.1.)

Managers, for example, will no doubt have to make presentations to their colleagues. You should find out how they go about making these presentations and, in particular, discuss the ways in which they influence others to get decisions made. The higher you go up in the organization, the more you have to build a political network in order to

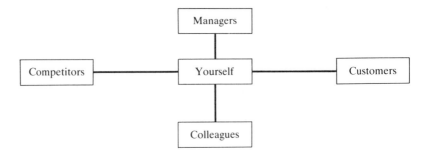

**Figure 8.1**  *The practical learning areas*

influence decision making. This is a key skill and can be learned by observing and talking over with managers what they do.

The second area is 'looking forward'. Typically, your managers will have to make decisions over a longer time span than you do. While you may have to worry about what is happening over the next two or three weeks, they are usually more concerned with what is happening over the next two or three years. You can, therefore, learn much by talking over with them how they begin to assess the various options and alternatives.

The third area is 'managing staff'. Typically, your managers will have wider responsibilities than you. You can learn much by finding out what their approach is to gaining staff commitment, motivation, loyalty and, of course, the key factor of improving performance. These are all topics which, if opened up in the appropriate way, can lead to a tremendous amount of learning.

One other key aspect of learning from other managers is that, usually, they have done a job which is similar, if not identical, to the one you are doing now. The learning should, therefore, be a two-way process. You should indicate to the managers that you are open to ideas and suggestions based upon their experience. Indeed, very often they have many good ideas but do not wish to foist them upon you for fear of interference. If you, however, indicate you are willing to listen and learn, then this will set up a mutual dialogue between you which can be of considerable benefit.

Do not wait, therefore, for the manager to come to help you. Take the initiative and find ways in which you can learn from him or her. This may require taking a risk at times but it will pay off well as you can begin to establish a relationship whereby you both work together and learn from each other's experience.

**How to learn from your manager**  I have learned a great deal from people to whom I have reported— much of it has been positive and some of it has been negative. I believe, however, that learning from the manager, whether it be in terms of what to do or what not to do, is very important. The good manager will try to show by example the ways in which the job can be done. This is what we would expect from someone who knows the job, but it does not always lead to effective management development. A manager may be so busy doing the job that other people do not realize how he or she is doing it.

If you want to learn from your manager, however, it is not only important to observe but also to question. Let the manager know that you are keen to learn and wish to discover why things are done in particular ways. Try to create an opportunity to find out the way in which the manager has tackled the job.

It is not always easy to do this because it can rarely be done in a formal meeting. It is best done perhaps informally, whether it be over lunch or maybe drinks. The Japanese seem to have devised an interesting way in which the manager can socialize with the team after work and such matters can be discussed in a more relaxed atmosphere. You may, therefore, need to take the initiative and invite the manager out for lunch or a drink and discuss the ways in which jobs are done.

Clearly this needs to be handled well because your manager may feel that you are moving on to territory that has not previously been open. If, however, you indicate that your intention is to learn rather than to criticize, and seek to discuss how things could be improved, this will usually take much of the suspicion out of such meetings.

## Learning from other organizations

Management is a competitive business. The reason is that we are invariably in a situation where other organizations are trying to produce the same product. If you want to improve your own management practice, it is wise to look at what other organizations are doing. This can be done both formally and informally.

At the informal level, it is useful to do a comparative analysis on a regular basis to see what your competitors are doing. Naturally, you will look at their prices, their advertising, and the products they are producing. Behind that, however, what processes are they adopting that will enable them to become more competitive than your company?

Over the last 10 years we have recognized that the Japanese organizations have been extremely effective in most areas in developing competitive products and services. That in itself is observable to anyone. What is less obvious, however, is the way in which they have gone about it. They have clearly been using superior management practices, in order to get the commitment and cooperation of their colleagues, to produce such high-quality products at such low cost.

We are now beginning, through various studies and discussions with the Japanese, to realize that this is not just something peculiar to their own culture. They have, above all, begun to develop managers who work in such a way that they can get superior results. Much of this clearly involves team management and bringing people together to discuss common problems, and developing solutions where there is a high degree of commitment.

We should, therefore, look at our competitors and see what they are doing. There are certain areas that they will keep hidden, but, in my experience, when it comes to management development, most companies are prepared to share openly what they do. Management development is not seen to be one of the secret areas.

## Intercompany studies

I have, therefore, organized a number of management development programmes around intercompany visits. Initially, there was a high degree of scepticism about this because it was believed that companies would not invite other companies, even on occasions in the same industry, to visit their premises. I have not, however, found this to be the case. Indeed, on the contrary, I have found most companies willing to accept visitors from other companies and to share information on the processes and ideas for improving their performance.

In one particular case, I asked a large company to identify the key areas in which they felt they needed to improve their performance. They identified profitability, productivity, quality, communication, cost control, safety and various other areas.

I then asked a number of the managers to meet, for a short workshop, to discuss how they could find out from others the way in which they were tackling similar problems. We decided to work in quartets and identify various companies who seemed to be doing particularly well in the areas mentioned.

Each of the quartets then began to work out how they would meet executives from those companies to talk over what they were doing and how they were doing it. Clearly, it was important that we did not have overlaps of people going to the same company. We therefore worked out a plan that would involve different people visiting organizations over a period of time. They then organized themselves and agreed that they would report back within two months.

When the time for the report workshop occurred, there was considerable energy, enthusiasm and excitement. The managers on their visits had learned an enormous amount. They had found their hosts in the other companies, in the main, welcoming and willing to talk through the way in which they were doing things. At the workshop they reported on what could be done and how it could be done.

Because the information they were relaying came from outside of their own company, it also had, I believe, a higher credibility. The important thing they found was that other companies had developed interesting practices but they needed to be converted to the particular culture in which they were operating. Nothing, therefore, was instantly transferable.

A key aspect of this project was that it facilitated management development in a most effective way. Managers were able to get outside their own job, their own organization and their own culture to look at the ways in which other people were doing things. They could then make positive recommendations for change. The programme was a major success and had particular impact not only on improving individual performance, but also on their organizational performance.

In your own management development, therefore, it may be wise to start with what other people are doing and see what you can learn from them.

**Learning from customers**

I was working with the senior management of a large manufacturing company. They were discussing the importance of becoming more customer orientated. For a considerable period they discussed how to improve marketing strategies. The phrase 'getting closer to the customer' came up often.

The production manager, who had not spoken during the meeting, leant forward and said that he did not feel he had much to contribute to the debate. One of the other managers asked him why. He said. 'Well I have worked here for 29 years. I've done most of the jobs in the factory, having started on the shop floor, and worked my way up through the various management positions. In the whole of the 29 years I can't ever remember a customer coming to visit me in the factory. Perhaps of more significance is the fact that I've never been to visit a customer. I've never been invited by any of our marketing or sales people to go and visit a customer and I haven't pressed to do so myself.'

There was a silence around the room. The production manager broke it by saying, 'We can talk a lot about our marketing orientation but unless it has an impact on people like myself and other people in all departments, then it won't mean much in practice.' The discussion then focused not upon grand strategies and theories and ideas, but upon the practicalities and how people could meet with and learn from customers.

In terms of executive development, customers form one of the most important sources of development. It is they who can give direct feedback on what is required. It is they who can indicate to managers how performance can be improved. It is they, above all, who can indicate what the future trends are going to be, in terms of purchasing and buying behaviour.

If you, therefore, want to develop as a manager, go and talk to the people who will ultimately make the major decision as to whether or not you and your colleagues have a job in the future—your customers. It is they who pay good money for the products and services that you produce. If you do not understand what your customers are thinking, then it is difficult to develop yourself and other people to meet their needs.

Some people say it is difficult to meet customers. They are busy people. In my experience, however, customers are always willing to state their views if approached in the right way. Many organizations are, increasingly, inviting customers on to their premises and providing hospitality and an opportunity to share ideas. Giving customers a walk around a factory may be important, but the real value is in creating an environment where people can discuss things and learn from each other. Never invite customers, therefore, unless you are really prepared in terms of having a set of questions and a conducive environment whereby they can talk to you freely.

Likewise, when you go to a customer's organization, ask for an opportunity to talk about what you can do to improve your performance, and your company's performance, to serve them better. They may be surprised but usually you will find that they can give you useful information, like tips and guidelines, that will enable you to become more effective.

Within your own organization, of course, there are people who meet the customers every day—the salespeople. Very often they are ignored in terms of the feedback they can provide. If, however, you want to improve as an executive and find out what customers are thinking, convene meetings with the salespeople so they can give you feedback.

In my experience, it is extremely valuable to have salespeople meet with people in accounts, in production, in personnel, in the distribution department and so on. Meet in small groups to discuss the way in which customers are thinking and reacting. The action, however, must always come back to what you, as a manager, will do differently and how you will develop yourself to keep ahead of the game. Customers are a potent source of information and ideas; they are the basis upon which all companies depend. It is for this reason that executive development should start with what customers, as much as any other group, are saying.

# Guidelines

We can all learn a great amount from others, providing we do it on an organized basis. Look, therefore, at your own approach and develop a plan to improve your own development.

### Colleagues

In what specialized professional areas do you wish to establish a greater understanding—finance?, commercial law?, marketing?, distribution?, production? Make a list of colleagues to whom you can talk, and visit them. They will normally be only too happy to talk to you about their work.

### Your manager

Let your manager know that you are interested in developing the skills and abilities that will take you on to the next level. Ask him, or her, what you will have to learn. Again, you will be surprised that most managers will be pleased you have sought out their experience. Indeed, they will no doubt also learn from the discussion.

### Other organizations

Arrange to see how other organizations work. It is not difficult. You will have social friends who work for a wide variety of organizations. Ask them if you can visit and find out how they operate. This can provide great insights and learning.

### Customers

Ask the customers to visit your organization and talk to you. Stew Leonard, who runs a family dairy business in Connecticut, USA, decided to do this and became famous for it when Tom Peters (1987) made a video and wrote of it in his books. Stew Leonard had, however, been learning from his customers for years before this. Maybe you should also visit your customers. I do this frequently. It is satisfying to find out what they do with the products and services you provide. It can give you inspiration for what you should do next.

What plans do you have, therefore, for:

- learning from your colleagues?
- learning from your manager?
- learning from other organizations?
- learning from your customers?

# 9 Individual development plans

*Men of superior mind, busy themselves first in getting to the roots of things; and when they have succeeded in this, the right course is open to them.*

Confucius

## Personal responsibility

Ultimately everyone is responsible for his or her own management development. If a person is not keen to improve the way he or she performs, it is unlikely that any advice will be heeded. I, therefore, put a great deal of effort into giving people an opportunity to identify what they personally are trying to do to improve their own development. This is where individual development plans are very important.

It is useful, at least once if not twice a year, to meet with members of the team and discuss their plans for making them more effective. These should be output-orientated meetings, in which the staff members indicate to you what they will do, when they will do it and how. If, however, they indicate they do not know the answer to any of these questions, then through the counselling interview you can give help and guidance where appropriate.

## Development plans

Let us reflect upon the issues raised by a member of my team at such an interview and consider how this could be the basis for effective management development. The discussion lasted about an hour and I asked the question, 'What do you personally wish to concentrate upon in order to become more effective as a manager?' The member had some very clear ideas in certain areas but other points were rather vague.

During the discussion she said, 'I have been thinking about trying to gather more knowledge about the processes of management and I have decided to register for the Master of Business Administration programme.' We discussed this and looked at the way in which it would help her to become more effective. We agreed that it was not the knowledge in itself that was important, but how it could be applied to the business situation. We, therefore, agreed that in each of the areas to be studied, we should look for project applications.

## Action contacts

My colleague also indicated that it would be valuable to attend a conference of the Librarians' Association for four days. Initially I was rather sceptical of this but asked how it could form part of the individual plan. She pointed out that librarians were the major source of information to help us in the development of our products—which were in the publishing field—and, in many cases, the key decision makers. She indicated that it was important to understand the way in which the librarians operated. I agreed that it would be a useful part of her personal development as well as relevant to the business. She, therefore, went to the librarians' conference on the understanding that she would write a report of the conference not only for herself but for the benefit of others.

**Job-related development**

Beyond these two points my colleague was rather vague as to what else she needed for individual development. We, therefore, discussed a number of points and the following key items began to emerge as important.

1 She indicated it would be useful to meet me on a quarterly basis to discuss her progress and issues, and this should probably be done in an informal environment—perhaps over a coffee or a lunch break.

2 We discussed particular projects in which she was involved and those that were more likely to stretch her and help cover new fields. We agreed, therefore, it would be useful for her to join an interdepartmental project.

3 When discussing the area of negotiation, it was realized that she had previously had little experience of this. As a considerable part of our business was, however, involved in developing joint ventures and taking over other businesses, it was agreed that she would read in this area and also join one of the negotiation teams.

4 The other area of individual development that came up strongly was that of marketing. She had not previously been involved in any marketing work but was increasingly having to do the market planning. It was agreed, therefore, that she should have the opportunity to meet with consultants in the field and talk over how we could improve our performance and her own particular performance.

5 The final point to emerge was that it would be useful to keep a record of achievement and a managerial log book on what was done and how it could be improved. This turned out to be a very useful proposal.

This, therefore, is one example of how individual development plans can be created through discussion. The important thing is not so much the plan but the discussion that surrounds the thinking of what should be done. Equally, it is important to have a follow-up meeting on a quarterly basis to consider the outcomes and reinforce the next steps.

Individual development should always have short-, medium- and long-term plans. In the case of the discussion with my colleague, going to the librarians' conference was the short-term aspect. In the medium term we agreed she should join various project groups and become involved in new kinds of work. The long-term aspect is clearly the MBA, which was going to take somewhere between three and four years on a part-time basis. It was, therefore, clear that my colleague had an individual development plan and I was able thereafter to support and encourage her in the achievement of the objectives.

Individual development planning, therefore, requires a considerable amount of counselling skill on behalf of the manager (see Figure 9.1).

```
┌─────────────────────────────────────────────────────────────┐
│            QUESTIONS A MANAGER SHOULD ASK                     │
│                                                               │
│   1  How best can I spend my time?                            │
│   2  Who else could/should be doing the work on my desk?      │
│   3  What am I improving and why?                             │
│   4  What am I for, what am I against?                        │
│   5  What are my special strengths and weaknesses?            │
│   6  What am I doing to develop the effectiveness of myself   │
│      and others?                                              │
│   7  What is the return v. risk of the objectives I pursue?   │
│   8  What have I learned in the last month?                   │
│   9  What motivates me most?                                  │
│  10  How many of my objectives do I achieve on time?          │
│  11  What is my action plan for one month, one year, five     │
│      years?                                                   │
└─────────────────────────────────────────────────────────────┘
```

*Figure 9.1   Counselling skill of the manager*

## Self-development

The acceptance of management development as being a personal responsibility, additional to anything that may be provided by your employing organization, has been well argued by Mike Pedler and his colleagues. They have identified various ways in which this can be done and applied the principles with individuals and organizations.

The emphasis clearly has to be on personal review and planning for one's own development. The next step is to share and compare with others so that you can learn how, from different examples. *A Manager's Guide to Self-Development* (Pedler *et al.* 1978) is an excellent guide to activities and opportunities.

The field for such development is now wide open, given the range of distance learning resources being developed and marketed by such organizations as The Open University in the UK, and others. The key, however, is finding a group of like-minded people who also wish to establish their own development programme. Theirs may be different from yours but you could help each other. Probably the best place for finding like-minded people is through your professional institute or association.

## How often should you change roles?

We can all learn a great deal by watching how other people do their jobs. We can, however, probably learn much more if we actually do that job ourselves. In my discussions with people who made it to the chief executive position I found that, on average, they were changing role every two and a half years. They were obviously people who were bright and able and, by moving from one challenging assignment to another, were gaining experience. In so doing they were also being developed as managers.

If, therefore, you wish to improve your own managerial skills consider how long you should be in any one role. If you have been in the same position for five years or more, this is probably too long. You will start jumping the same fences for the second or third time. You may make fewer mistakes, but you probably will not learn very much.

It is particularly important for people who have technical backgrounds, such as engineers or accountants, to get outside those technical areas in their early thirties. Otherwise, they will never learn anything of significance about other business operations such as marketing, project management, distribution, finance and other key aspects of the business.

If your own organization is not arranging excellent job moves to provide you with experience, you should probably plan your own. This may mean leaving the organization, or applying for positions within different divisions. It comes back to the point about taking control of your own career and managing your own destiny.

To learn, you need the challenge of new jobs. If you stay too long in one job you will have a depth of understanding, but unless it is a general management job it will be relatively narrow in scope.

My view is that being in a managerial job for less than three years does not give enough time to achieve very much or to see tasks through to a conclusion. However, I also feel that if you stay more than five years, it is usually too long.

Rosemary Stewart (1984) conducted a study with the International Thompson organization on managers who made job moves, and particularly those making radical job moves. She concluded that the important factors in a successful transition are (a) a good briefing prior to taking up the appointment and (b) an experienced person to act as mentor once you have taken the job.

The important point, however, is that if you really want to develop as a manager, do not stay in one job too long. In my own career, I have moved five times in 25 years. On reflection, I should probably have moved seven times and gained more practical experience earlier in a direct profit or loss situation in a small company, and also taken on a major internal advisory role within a large company.

Therefore, consider your own job moves. How would you assess your career so far?

1 Have the job moves been well planned?
2 What did you learn from them?
3 What other job moves do you feel you need to extend your management development experience?

One way to review your career is to place the job changes you have had in a matrix (see Figure 9.2).

## Changing roles

This, for most people, is the most difficult transition. Many times I have heard of the first-class engineer who has difficulty becoming a good manager. The same is true of many research scientists, or top salespeople. The reason is, of course, that managing is a different job.

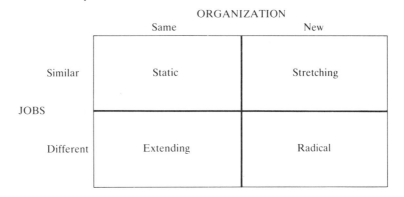

**Figure 9.2** *Matrix of possible job changes*

You may need to know about the technical content in order to speak the language but the management aspect is a process involving finance, marketing, planning, and coordinating people.

Laurence Peter made himself famous by suggesting we all rise to the level of our incompetence (Peter and Hull 1969). There is some truth in the principle but we can stave off the evil day by developing ourselves. This, in my view, requires a continuing attention to one's own management development and you should set goals and plans for this just as much as you do for producing and selling the products of your organization.

**Taking the initiative**

Until recently, most people awaited the 'call from above'. It was assumed that, if you were loyal to an organization, someone would look after your interests and provide opportunities. This philosophy, while still prevailing in Japan, is now breaking down in western organizations and people today recognize that there is a free market in which they can move to secure experience.

**Acting positions**

There are a variety of ways in which you can organize job moves without necessarily leaving your organization. Some organizations, particularly the public service, provide alternatives on a regular basis by establishing what is called an 'acting position'. This means, in essence, that when a senior manager is on leave or seconded to some other work, a person is put into that position and takes over that office with all responsibilities in the acting role. In certain cases, this tandem position can continue for some time and is used as a device to avoid making a decision on a permanent replacement. In my experience, however, it is usually a good way of enabling people to gain experience and testing them in a job before they are formally selected for it.

**Secondments**

The secondment approach is also well worth doing. This is particularly prevalent in organizations that have high emphasis on project management. Here, people are asked to take on specific assignments such as joining the new product launch team for a period of time. Another approach is, perhaps, to help establish a joint venture overseas and people are seconded to those jobs. All of these are excellent learning and development opportunities and should not be missed, despite the fact that they cause upheaval and have a high degree of uncertainty about them, due to their temporary nature.

**Exchanges**  Some organizations favour exchange programmes. This is where people from one organization, or department, swap jobs with another person for a period of time ranging usually from three months to one year. Again, if properly managed, it is a valuable way of gaining experience. Unfortunately, in my view, too many of these interchange programmes are very badly managed. They just move people from one work area to another and entail 'jumping in the deep end of the pool' without much guidance or support.

I recommend to organizations using exchange programmes that they bring all the participants together on a regular basis so that they can learn from each other. I favour initially getting all participants together for a two-day workshop in which they agree among themselves the objectives that they will pursue on the interchange programme. They are then asked to keep a record of what they do and what they learn and to meet regularly, either monthly or bimonthly in workshops, to share their learnings. In this way, there is a systematic approach towards development, and outputs can be assessed and measured. It also enables the participants themselves to look sharper in focusing not only upon what they are doing, but upon what they are learning.

**Rotations**  Other organizations are highly disciplined about job moves. The military, for example, have specific postings where people are moved from job to job and area to area on a schedule. The banks also have been known to establish a similar system, whereby branch managers have been moved from town to town on a three- or five-year cycle. This can be very disruptive of family life, of course, where children have to move from school to school and new homes have to be found.

Increasingly, organizations are finding it difficult to get people to accept these regular moves, particularly when both man and wife are working. Nevertheless, it is a system designed to improve the management skills and abilities by giving ever-widening experience. Overall, there is much to be said for job moves.

# Representing the organization

From time to time, requests come in from schools, or community groups, for someone to make a presentation about the work of your organization. Such requests will usually end up in the Public Relations Department, or the equivalent. Some professional PR person is despatched to give the same speech they have given many times before.

Why not see such requests as a major development opportunity? Ask staff from various levels if they are interested in representing the organization. Help them prepare. Provide them with some publicity material and let them loose. They will do their best, learn a great deal and probably do a good job.

Indeed, why wait to be asked? Your organization should be pro-active and let it be known that your staff will be willing to present an up-to-date picture on what you do, how you do it and the benefits. This is not a social service; it is good public relations and a part of the marketing campaign. Moreover, it is sound management development, if it enables people to communicate more effectively. Who knows, the people most convinced by the communication may be the presenters themselves, in so far as it enhances their confidence.

Numerous organizations, of course, do this and computer companies such as IBM, APPLE, Hewlett Packard and others spend a great deal of time in this way but, often, it is the 'professionals', not those who are developing, who do it. Banks are becoming more aware of the need to communicate and many of them now encourage their local branch managers to be involved in presenting to local bodies.

Government organizations, of course, need to keep close to their paymasters, the public. Unfortunately, too many bureaucrats sit behind their desks rather than get out to present their services and, in the process, miss a major management development learning opportunity.

**Experience moves**    Some young people regard the first 15 years of their working life, after they have completed their training, as a series of learning experiences. Young graduates, for example, may spend three years with ICI, followed by another three years with Kodak, followed by three years with General Electric and then another three years with Mobil. This is all a far cry from the traditional Japanese model where employees are expected to stay with one firm all their lives and have their careers managed for them in a series of job moves. Increasingly, however, in western organizations, managers are taking their management development into their own hands and this involves moving either between organizations or within the organization on a regular basis.

Job moves are not, however, in themselves sufficient. Alongside the job moves must go real learning and development and this, in my view, requires a planned approach, where people are brought together to identify not only what they have done, but what they have learned and how they have applied it. In this way, experience can be made to pay.

**External development**    Much management development occurs outside the paid employment situation. I always remember a senior manager complaining that he wished one of his subordinates would put as much effort into his full-time job as he did into that of being secretary of the local musical society. Maybe many of the skills being learned in the evening were not being called upon during the day.

We all have opportunities beyond what is offered at work. The only limitation is our time, energy and the cost of getting involved. Figure 9.3 overleaf, gives some options you may wish to consider.

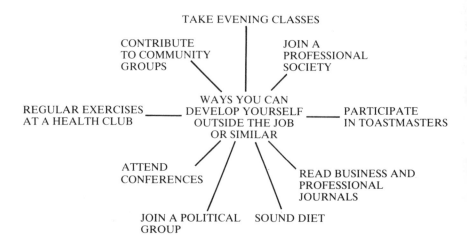

**Figure 9.3**  *Other management development activities*

## Management development and acting

While in a meeting with Barry Smith, who at that time was the Director of Human Resources for ACI Ltd, we were discussing many of the managerial issues he was facing, including industrial relations disputes, the selection of high-calibre managerial talent, the development of younger people, and other matters concerned with productivity and safety. We reflected on the different roles that a manager has to play in order to succeed and the words of William Shakespeare, when he said, '. . . one man in his time plays many parts' came to us.

We concluded that Shakespeare had many wise things to say about management and decided to look at some of his other great sayings. The result was that we eventually wrote a book called *Shakespeare and Management* (Margerison and Smith 1988), based upon quotations from Shakespeare, which seemed to be relevant today. The key point, however, is, that Shakespeare recognized that we all have to play various roles in order to succeed and, in particular, do so in the work situation.

In our day-to-day work, although we do not set out to be actors, we nevertheless have to take on different aspects of the job. At various times we have to listen and be sympathetic when people have personal problems. At other times we have to be logical and analytical when assessing a business proposition, and be strong and tough when negotiating. There are yet other times when we have a joke and see the lighter side of life.

Each day, people are continually watching and assessing how well we do the job. This is not only in terms of technical competence but in the way we actually perform in the role. A senior manager who was very good at his work was passed over, as one colleague said, 'because he can't relate with other people'. Another person who was very sound technically was also passed over because he had, as the committee felt, a disinclination to 'go out and seek new opportunities and develop a business'.

Now these are not just personal comments about people's personalities.

They reflect something about the way in which the individual takes on, or does not take on, roles. There may be more comments about a person's ability to learn. Very often I have found that managers do not even recognize the roles they are playing. Increasingly, more and more work is being directed towards helping managers develop their roles, although many managers do not like the notion that they are being trained as actors.

Ian Mangham (1986) has made a particular study of this facet of managerial life and has indicated that there is a drama taking place in all organizations. People do have roles and scripts and there are villains and victims, heroes and rescuers, and a host of other fascinating interactions.

For this purpose of management development, however, it is vitally important that managers learn how to take on and adapt to various situations. This means taking on a job and learning the wide range of roles that go with that job.

Some of the most important roles that I have worked out with managers have been listed below. Some are well established but new roles are emerging and we need to recognize this in our management development work.

**Key managerial roles**

- *The marketeer* Managers have to be more market driven—find ways of listening to customers.
- *The politician* Managers have to develop political skills—find ways of building alliances and networks to ensure you and your group get resources.
- *The communicator* Managers have to be top communicators—develop skills of enquiry, diagnosis and summarizing to understand others, as well as proposing and directing so people understand you.
- *The team linker* Managers have to develop effective teams that can compete—look to sports teams.
- *The self-manager* Managers need to manage themselves (not too much strain) and their time.
- *The profit maker* Managers need to achieve business objectives on time and to high quality.
- *The negotiator* Managers need to learn how to make relevant decisions and say 'no' or 'yes' for the good of the business, not for an easy life.
- *The psychologist* Managers need to understand people's behaviour—to be a full-time managerial psychologist.
- *The actor* Managers need to play many roles—the negotiator, sales person, counsellor, planner, representative, etc.
- *The educator* Managers need to help others to develop their skills and enhance their potential through assigning challenging work.
- *The salesman* All managers need to learn how to present and sell their ideas.

It is possible to learn how to take on these roles. It is just not a matter of gathering knowledge, but also skills through practice. The first stage is to become aware of how effective or ineffective you are in those roles; the second stage is to go out and gather some knowledge based on practice; the third stage is to get some feedback from trying things out; and the fourth stage is to improve your performance.

The list of roles identified above increasingly recognizes the key aspects of managerial work. They go beyond those originally identified by Mintzberg (1975) and others. They are the basis for successful performance, and the sooner managers recognize that in their own management development they need to find ways of performing these roles at a high level of competence on the organizational stage, the better they will be doing their job.

## Guidelines

Individual development is, above all, a personal matter and, therefore, primarily your own responsibility. To succeed, you need to plan your personal self-development in the same way you would plan any business activity:

- Set yourself objectives.
- Obtain resources.
- Set a timetable.
- Get into action.
- Measure the results.
- Apply what you have learned.
- Try again and again.

# 10 Do you have any movers and shakers?

*Before everything else, getting ready is the secret of success.*

Henry Ford

## High-energy people

I often see advertisements in the executive recruitment pages asking people who are 'self-starters' or have 'entrepreneurial skills' to apply for jobs. Equally, when I am visiting companies, I am often introduced to people who have been described by their colleagues as 'whizz kids' or 'fast trackers'.

These people are regarded as being exceptionally talented achievers. The people concerned: (a) are usually bright, highly energetic, and often unconventional in the way in which they conduct business; (b) invariably work with a strong sense of intuition as to what needs to be done to succeed; and, above all, (c) have the drive and determination to see things through to effective action.

Such people are often at an early stage in their career, and are rather impatient of others who do not seem to move at the same pace. They may, therefore, create conflict from time to time as they try to move forward, often short-circuiting many of the processes and procedures and consultative practices. They believe they can justify their behaviour through the results they achieve, and very often do so. These people are the movers and the shakers of an organization.

The question I am often asked is, 'How do you manage such people and how do you create others who will produce similar results, albeit in a more conventional fashion?' Many organizations have turned towards the assessment centre as a way of identifying the future movers and shakers of an organization. Movers and shakers, however, usually identify themselves regardless of any formal procedures. They are, by definition, the action men and women of the organization. They have a strong sense of direction and will create a lot of heat and, occasionally, some light in the pursuit of their objectives.

## How to encourage initiative

The question from a management development point of view is 'How can we encourage such people and, at the same time, channel their efforts so that they are congruent with the overall organizational aims?'

- First, do not put such people on formal long courses where they are taken off the job. That will only slow them down and take them away from where they are really effective.
- Second, do not surround them with too many rules and regulations or too many forms that have to be filled, in order to comply with the

system. That will only frustrate them and lead to more deviant behaviour.

- Third, do not have them reporting to managers who are unsympathetic to new ideas, are rather bureaucratic in their practices, and prefer an easy life at the top.

**Forums for reviewing moving and shaking**

The answer, in terms of management development for movers and shakers, is to move with them in the spirit they bring to the job. Rather than letting them run free, they should be given challenging assignments with specific outputs and time schedules and asked to report on a regular basis to a forum of their peers, as well as their superiors, on the progress that they are making.

Such an environment will ensure that their ideas are subjected to the closest scrutiny, in a positive and challenging way, by other movers and shakers. They, therefore, will have to make public what they are doing and have others comment upon it and criticize it. This peer review process is a superb vehicle for sharpening the wits and professional practice of people who may, from time to time, be inclined to act before sufficient thought has taken place.

By creating a forum in which the movers and the shakers have to report to each other, they will begin to consider and think through the issues in advance. No one wants to look a fool in front of people whom they respect. In a competitive environment, the movers and shakers will quickly get the message that their future lies in their ability to communicate and convince others of a similar and higher level in the organization, as well as in their ability to bring home the gold at the end of the day.

**The Harold Geneen system**

Harold Geneen became world renowned for his ability to set up such a forum. He insisted that all his managers reported in to him at regular meetings on their achievements and plans. Before each meeting, he would insist that they forward documents with detailed information, particularly on the quantitative aspects of their work.

He would then go through these documents thoroughly and, in front of everyone, question the managers on exactly what they had done, what they were doing and what they intended to do. If managers could not substantiate their arguments with fact, he would send them forth to get the exact detail.

He once sent round a memo to all his managers, which read as follows:

The highest art of professional management requires the literal ability to smell a real fact from all others—and moreover to have the temerity, intellectual curiosity, guts and/or plain impoliteness, if necessary, to be sure that what you do have is indeed what we will call an 'unshakeable fact'. (Geneen and Moscow 1984).

He valued movers and shakers who could manage autonomous units. He moved and shook them. He wanted movers and shakers who could plan and deliver based on a hard-nosed result-based accounting system.

# Assessment or development centres

It has been said that you can identify movers and shakers by having them attend an assessment centre. I do not like assessment centres. They are false ways of coming to judgements about a person. It is the equivalent of judging a cricketer by how he performs at the nets. Much time and effort, however, have gone into establishing the artificial conditions on which assessments are made. The British Civil Service led the way and others, mistakenly, felt the principles should be applied to industry.

The general theory is, that an assessment centre can, through a battery of psychological tests and simulated tasks, provide enough data on a person to indicate certain levels of management potential. This may, or may not be so. Bray (1974) and his colleagues, from their extensive work at the American AT&T company, argues that he has evidence to show you can increase the probability of identifying those who will 'make it'.

This is fine, if you are assessing new recruits to a company. You may need such extra data to justify putting someone in a job that will be demanding. My concern is that it is no way to treat existing staff. It is certainly not a way to treat movers and shakers. They should be assessed doing a real job, making money for the company.

After a person has worked in a company for, say, a year, there could be a need to assess if they have potential for future advancement. An assessment centre, however, for such a person is an inappropriate trial. However, such centres may have an important role in self-development and personal understanding. The individual in such cases, however, must be the sole recipient of the data feedback and the event should not be conducted by a member of the company who could influence the future career of the person in question.

In contrast, I am in favour of development centres. These are workshops designed to enable people to assess themselves and learn new skills. Movers and shakers may learn some useful tips if the centre is focused into how to convert their energy into team action.

You may ask, 'What is the difference between an assessment centre and a development centre.' The first is there for others to make an assessment of peoples' potential in an off-the-job situation. The second is there to foster and develop new skills and abilities. There is a world of difference in meaning, and movers and shakers will soon see the difference.

For whose benefit is an assessment centre conducted? If a person volunteers to be 'assessed', then that is his or her free choice. My advice to organizations is, however, do not waste your money setting up an expensive in-house assessment centre. If individuals want to be assessed, you can send them to an external agency on a one-off basis, where you do not have to pay the overheads. If, however, you want to provide off-the-job development, then this is best achieved by working on real tasks rather than doing simulations. Development centres can therefore be made practical and useful by ensuring that they develop people to work more effectively on real tasks.

## Women in management

This has been a topic of considerable interest over the last decade or two. Prior to that point, it was traditional for women to take employment until they were married and then resign to manage the home and have children. With the advent of wider tertiary education for women, there are now, in many universities, more women students than men. Furthermore, women now plan for a career rather than become home managers on a full-time basis. This sociological trend has had a major impact on society and particularly the role structure within management and the home.

We have not seen as many women as movers and shakers, but we shall shortly do so. Women are increasingly taking the opportunities to show what they can do. To what extent should there be special management programmes for women? Given the principles of antidiscrimination and equal opportunity, there should be no need for special programmes, and existing programmes should be designed to include the same opportunities for women in terms of selection and resource allocation.

Management, as a set of skills, can be acquired equally by men or women. It is the culture of organizations—in terms of promotion practices, reward systems, attitudes and the traditions—that needs to change. Management development policies, therefore, need to reflect equal opportunity. Regular audits should be conducted by action learning groups of both male and female managers working together to ensure that the policies are practised.

This will ensure that justice is seen to be done and that people are treated on their merits rather than on their sex. Organization life is a competition. We should not bend over backwards to distort the race by having a token woman on the Board or promoted to a particular level. Providing the opportunities are there for everyone to participate, and people are judged fairly on their performance, then women will develop as managers and be appointed as such.

Already a number of women have made their mark as movers and shakers, such as Laura Ashley and Steve Shirley in business, while in politics Mesdammes Thatcher, Bhutto, Ghandi and Aquino have shown what can be done. Others will follow and men need to adjust to women who will take a front seat in the changing organization.

## Competition and cooperation

Management development for the movers and shakers is just as important as for those who might have a more steady and predictable career. Indeed, in many respects, it is more important. Such people can easily go off the rails if they do not have some guidance on how to improve. The organization should therefore provide opportunities for the movers and shakers to learn with and from each other.

- Encourage them to compete in a cooperative way by sharing and comparing what they are doing.
- Provide opportunities for them to help and consult each other so that they can perhaps visit each others' territories and learn some of the tricks that they are able to implement, in order to secure bigger and better profits.

• If the movers and shakers are so clever, then they should be able to help each other learn how to do the job better.

## Limited risks

Movers and shakers can create problems as well as successes. They typically have a higher willingness to take a risk—some would say a gamble. The company, therefore, needs to insure against such risks.

As part of the management development effort, why not set up a small or medium liability company and let them try out their ideas? It may be expensive but the returns could be well worth it. You will need to provide a senior manager (perhaps one who has just retired) as a mentor and friendly consultant to ensure that there is an 'old head' alongside the enthusiasm and energy supplied by the mover and the shaker.

Above all, the mentor should have to account personally for what the movers and shakers do by providing a record of

• what they learned;
• how they helped others learn the business to continue when they leave;
• the financial results achieved;
• the strategic planning for future growth.

One example of this is John Scully (1988), who was a senior manager with Pepsi-Cola before becoming the chief executive of the Apple Corporation. He described himself as a workaholic who aimed to move and shake the organization. He said, 'I developed a reputation for being insensitive. At the time I failed to understand the importance of teamwork.'

He said, however, Chuck Mangold acted as a guide and mentor. He gave him advice on how to handle the personal and political issues. This is often required by movers and shakers who want to achieve their goal without always assessing the consequences. In the long run managers need to develop a network that has more friends than enemies.

## The Executive Connection

This organization was founded in the USA but is now extending its operation to other countries. It is a forum whereby chief executives can meet once a month with other people doing similar jobs. TEC, as the organization is called, attracts many movers and shakers who are able to save information and ideas and learn from each other.

We need similar such forums in large corporations so that the movers and shakers can test out their ideas on others of similar mould.

## Retaining the movers and shakers

It is vitally important, as part of the total management development process, that you hold on to your successful movers and shakers. Surround them, therefore, with systems that encourage them to perform. This obviously means creating flexible reward systems so they can share in the increased value they are creating. It also means providing resources to enable them to do what they are good at, rather than having to waste time on detailed administration.

---

### RUNNING THE SHOW

**Many movers and shakers ultimately want their own organizations. Some of them who have in various ways succeeded, are:**

**Robert Maxwell, who was a refugee from Hungary. He saw the opportunity in publishing and established Pergamon Press which started him off on a major business career.**

**Michael Marks was a refugee from Russia in the 1880s, who fled to England. He could not speak, read or write English, nor did he have any money or trade, but he formed, through his moving and shaking, the great Marks and Spencer stores.**

**Aristotle Onassis started from humble beginnings to build up a fleet of ships, to own Greek Islands and to marry the ex-wife of an American President.**

**Charles Forte, son of an Italian who emigrated to Scotland, saw his father and other relatives managing small shops. He decided to enlarge the business and ended up managing Trusthouse Forte, one of the world's large hotel chains.**

**Alan Bond started as a sign writer who found a talent in the property business, and became a multi-millionaire sponsoring the Australian team to win the Americas Cup.**

**Steve Jobs left school early and set up his business in a garage to develop a new computer concept that became the Apple MacIntosh and formed one of the world's major computer corporations.**

**Richard Branson, against the odds, broke into music publishing to establish Virgin Records and now also owns an airline.**

**Andrew Carnegie, born in Dunfermline to a poor Scottish crofter, emigrated to the USA where he read profusely and studied the stock market. He was to become the owner of the largest steel company of its day.**

*It is interesting to note that none of these people had any formal business training but learned from experience how to build profitable operations.*

---

It means above all, providing an environment within which they are encouraged to take risks but only within structures that have been assessed in a thorough but creative manner, in discussion with their peers and superiors. In this way, you will begin to get the best from your movers and shakers.

Along the way, ask them to document what they are doing. They may not like it or indeed thank you for it, but it is important that others learn from their achievements. It is vital, therefore, that they be asked to write a case study of why things went right and why things went wrong. These cases should form the basis for other managers whom you are trying to develop as movers and shakers, and the individual who wrote the case should lead the discussion. All of this provides for important learning in an organization. In the process, the movers and shakers will probably learn as much, if not more, than everyone else.

# Guidelines

Every organization needs people who will question and change the status quo in a positive, energetic way, rather than through negative criticism. Look, therefore, for movers and shakers. Do not be surprised if they challenge you and sometimes scare you with their wild ideas.

The foundation of this is a forum for movers and shakers so they can learn from each other. Ideas without a plan and facts to support intuition will be but a gamble. Management development can foster the creative talent of movers and shakers and help them become more successful by learning from their experiences as well as from others.

Some useful actions are to

- provide real opportunities where movers and shakers can test if they can make a profit;
- bring movers and shakers together in an organized way so they can learn from each other;
- ensure that movers and shakers report with real facts on their performance;
- reward movers and shakers only if they succeed, not for promises;
- link their management education to their business activity;
- ensure that movers and shakers develop balanced teams to support their entrepreneurial drive.

# 11 Management development counselling and advisory meetings

*Every real thought on every subject knocks the wind out of somebody or other.*
Oliver Wendell Holmes

A key part of management development is counselling. It is where the major part of the on-the-job development is done. It requires considerable interpersonal skills, and these will be identified in this chapter with guidelines for action.

Counselling is not a review or an appraisal process. It is an on-going part of the day-to-day work. A manager, when acting in a counselling role, is also being a consultant. It is, therefore, very important to observe some key principles of consultancy, if one wishes to be successful in counselling.

## Listen for cues and clues

When people need advice, or help, they will indicate the areas by the clues and cues they offer. Listen particularly for use of the words 'I', 'me', or 'my', as this is a key to their personal concerns. Particularly listen for emotional words such as 'worried', 'disappointed', 'upset', or 'happy'. These are key areas to be followed up by questions on why they feel that way. It may be just by listening that you enable the other person to solve his or her problems, but if not, you may need to give advice.

First of all, provide information and guidance that is specific and relevant to the task at hand. It is much easier to learn if somebody indicates to you in precise terms what you are doing wrong and how to improve it. It is no use waiting until a long time afterwards. The counselling has to take place when the person is aware of what is happening. If, for example, the reports that a person is producing are too long, or are lacking in certain factual areas, then it is wise to provide feedback on what you require. Indicate the solution, not just the problem.

## Time and place

Another key point about counselling and consulting is to ensure that the feedback is given to the individual at a time and place he, or she, can absorb it. It is not very appropriate to start counselling in a busy, noisy office, particularly if you are trying to correct someone's approach to work. They may feel embarrassed that any errors should be pointed out publicly. It is, therefore, best to counsel people quietly on the side.

This may mean that you ask them to meet you privately in your office or on some neutral territory to discuss methods.

Another key role of counselling is to help people to improve what they do well rather than just tell them negatively what they have done wrong. Phrase your counselling, therefore, in such a way that you indicate 'it would be helpful if you did . . .' or 'well I would like you to do . . .'

## Process consultation

The examples given above may imply that counselling is very much a solution-centred activity. In reality, it may not be so. Sometimes the best form of counselling is to have people diagnose for themselves what is going wrong.

It is this form of counselling that Edgar Schein (1969) has called *Process Consultation*. The prime effort is directed towards asking questions to enable people to become aware of what they are doing wrong. At this point, they can then begin to assess whether they know how to develop or acquire the solution themselves.

This may not always be so, and it is on those occasions that, if you have experience, you need to move into the solution-centred role of counselling.

### Purpose and process

Counselling is an extremely delicate issue. There is a danger that you may be stepping in too quickly before people have had a chance to find out for themselves. On the other hand, if you do not make a move to try to correct what you know from experience to be inappropriate behaviour, then you may have major problems on your hands. It is for these reasons that it is very important that you explain to the individual the purpose of the counselling.

Rather than just say 'do this' or 'do that', it is best to indicate initially why you feel it would be useful to talk the matter over. Wherever possible, try to refer to yourself rather than to them. Say, 'in order for me to get all the information in on time it would be helpful if you . . .'. This gives an indication of why you are about to counsel people.

### Convert general comment to specific examples

If a person says, 'I feel I'm not making progress in this job, it is difficult to get cooperation from people', this is a very strong cue and clue. At this point it is best in your counselling to make a request, rather than a statement. Rather than give them advice, ask them a question to find out more about why they find it difficult to get cooperation.

Usually in the early stages of such a meeting people talk in generalities. It is your job to get them to talk in specifics. You can do this if you avoid judgement and show that you wish to understand. Probe, therefore, without prying. For example, you can say, 'why do you say that?' or 'can you tell me a little bit more?'. Both of these are invitations and give the other person permission to perhaps say something he or she regarded as rather risky. The person can then provide specific examples, which you should work on to improve.

**Problem- and solution-centred approaches**

You will be counselling well if people say things to you that perhaps they previously would have kept to themselves. The issues then becomes discussable. It also enables the release of energy so that individuals can begin to think positively of their options and ideas.

When counselling, therefore, it is usually best to start with what I call a problem-centred approach. This involves enquiring and diagnosing as to why there is a problem. I have developed (Margerison 1987) a model to show the skills involved (see Figure 11.1). You can then move to summarize, without implying that you agree or disagree with what was said. Thereafter, you can move towards solutions by either asking the individuals themselves to propose what they think should be done, or you can suggest options.

It is by following the simple rules of enquiry, diagnosing, summarizing and proposing that you can begin to make progress. In doing so, you will not only be helping the individuals but will be enabling them to come to terms with issues about the management of their own job and career. Successful counselling activity enables someone who is having difficulties become effective and move from relatively low productivity to a higher level of productivity. Counselling is a key skill for all managers, particularly in the on-going management development process.

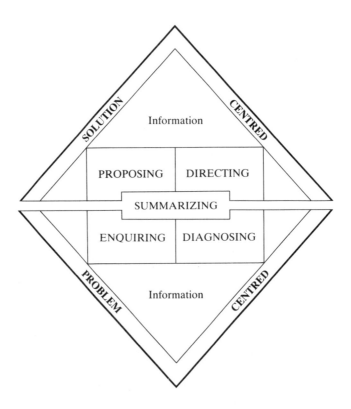

**Figure 11.1** *Interpersonal Management Skills (IMS) (Margerison, 1987).*

---

**WHEN TO COUNSEL**

There are numerous opportunities, such as when a subordinate says in a meeting, 'I'm having difficulty fitting everything in, given the lack of time.' Maybe he or she is managing time badly. Before giving solutions, however, find out what is meant by such key words as 'difficulty'.

On another occasion, you may see a colleague make a poor presentation. You can help by seeing the colleague afterwards, privately, and letting him or her know how you received the presentation and, if it seems right, offering positive ideas for improvement.

A colleague who is telling you of a success or failure with which he or she has been involved can be counselled if you start by asking what he or she learned from the experience and what he or she will do differently next time.

---

Knowing where you want to go and how to get there is the key to all management development activity. The job of the manager is to enable people to think through what they are going to do, in a practical way, and make sure that the ideas are translated into practice. Counselling, therefore, is a key skill in facilitating improvement at work.

Counselling is a support process and is designed primarily to enable others to come to conclusions, rather than to enable you to give them unsolicited advice. There is a time for both, but the essence of counselling is to help people diagnose their own problems and opportunities and reach solutions to which they personally feel committed.

# Learning from others

Managers counsel others in various ways. Sometimes it is by example. Other times, it is by writing. Sometimes, it is just by what they do. Managerial learning is often at its most effective when you are observing what others do and seeing how you could do likewise in your own job. Some may call it 'the comparative method' or simply 'copying', but it does not matter as long as it works for you. I have learned much from other managers and here are a few of the points for reference.

1 'Manage the cash and the profit will look after itself.' This was the view of one colleague. He continually kept an eye on the till, as he called it. He introduced tight cash management controls and limits so that 'we will stay afloat'. It was a great lesson and I use it now.

2 'You must prepare and read the papers before the meeting.' A simple enough point—but early in my career I tended more towards action than planning. I now recognize that a successful meeting requires twice as much work before the meeting. I now regularly ask my colleagues to write short papers to present to the meetings so that everyone, particularly themselves, is clear on what is required. I then have someone do 'notes of understanding' after the meeting.

3 Another colleague has a different approach. 'I write the minutes of the meeting before it has happened.' You cannot do that, I remarked,

'Well I have, and if anything else turns up, we can change them.' This colleague was not being arrogant. He had, however, clearly thought through what he wanted to happen. It concentrated his mind on the outputs.

4  Another person, who taught me about outputs, was Bill Reddin. We met many years ago when he was a visiting faculty member at Bradford Management Centre. He argued then, as he does now, that far too much emphasis is put on developing managerial systems that are based on inputs, rather than outputs. He is right. Ask yourself, and others, what you and they have achieved rather than what the job is.

5  'Business is about contracts,' said one of my colleagues, 'and that is what you need to learn.' Some of them will be written and others will be so-called 'understandings'. The important point, however, is establishing an agreement. Look for what will satisfy both of you, and then hold to it.

Early in my career, a colleague came to see me at my home. It was a pleasant summer's evening, so we sat outside. Over a drink, he pulled out some papers relating to an area of my work. He said that the ideas were good but to gain action I should write a budget. I objected, saying that this was the finance department's job. He persuaded me that it was mine. Since then I have recognized the value of budgeting as a planning tool, a decision-making method, a financial-measuring rod, a personal commitment and a set of expectations. It was a valuable lesson.

I have tended to learn by watching and talking to others. Perhaps the most important thing I have learned, however, is to take the viewpoint of the customers and imagine how they will respond. That then enables me to consider what we should do to improve the way we serve them.

I hope colleagues can learn something from me that will aid their development. I tend to use a whiteboard and a marker pen to illustrate ideas and summarize points during a meeting. I find it helpful and hope that others will learn how to gain clarification and agreement and then take effective action. As a quick checklist, (see Figure 11.2) write down what you have learned from others and what you hope colleagues will learn from you.

# Managing meetings

This is a skill often taken for granted and therefore not considered an important area for development. Research, into the managerial time spent at meetings has shown that, in some areas, to be as high as 80 or 90 per cent. It is an area of work where a great deal of consulting and advice is done in public, and often done badly.

It is interesting to note that the 3M Company in the USA has established a special Meetings Institute devoted to the study and improvement of meetings. Managers are guided and tutored in how to improve their skills.

This is not surprising, given some recent research by Green and Lazarus (1988). They studied over 1,000 executives to establish what they regarded as an effective meeting. A meeting was defined as a gathering of three or more participants for more than 15 minutes.

| *What I have learned from others*: | *What I hope others will learn from me*: |
|---|---|
| 1 ............................................... ............................................... | 1 ............................................... ............................................... |
| 2 ............................................... ............................................... | 2 ............................................... ............................................... |
| 3 ............................................... ............................................... | 3 ............................................... ............................................... |
| 4 ............................................... ............................................... | 4 ............................................... ............................................... |
| 5 ............................................... ............................................... | 5 ............................................... ............................................... |
| 6 ............................................... ............................................... | 6 ............................................... ............................................... |
| 7 ............................................... ............................................... | 7 ............................................... ............................................... |
| 8 ............................................... ............................................... | 8 ............................................... ............................................... |
| 9 ............................................... ............................................... | 9 ............................................... ............................................... |

**Figure 11.2**  *Managerial development checklist*

They found some vital information. First, the most unproductive meetings were reported in the finance area, that human resources meetings were notorious for not starting on time and that even in the best run meetings, which were attributed to general management, 30 per cent of the time was unproductive.

They concluded that managers have to concentrate on six key activities:

- preparing in advance and sharing of data
- circulating and agreeing agendas
- starting meetings on time
- staying on track
- achieving objectives of the meeting
- summarizing the outcomes in writing.

It was found that less than 10 per cent of meetings covered all these areas. Where meetings were successful, there was a greater use of visual aids. They concluded that it was not a lack of experience but a lack of training and systems that caused the failures. Managers with a great deal of experience still did not run effective meetings.

They concluded, however, that 'meetings are management'. Meetings affect the way people judge their managers. They set the tone of expectation for operations.

According to Green and Lazurus: 'If you can't manage a meeting, you can't manage.' Less than one-third of those surveyed, however, had any training in how to run a meeting. One of the keys to effective management development lies in developing a manager's skill in conducting

## A FATHER'S ADVICE

The following 15 points of advice, it is said, were written by William Marriott Sr for his son, J. W. Marriott Jr, president of Marriott Corporation which runs a chain of five-star hotels around the world.

Which, if any, of the following would you change in giving advice to your children?

1 Keep physically fit, and mentally and spiritually strong.

2 Guard your habits—bad ones will destroy you.

3 Pray about every difficult problem.

4 Study and follow professional management principles. Apply them logically and practically to your organization.

5 People are No.1—their development, loyalty, interest, and team spirit. Develop managers in every area. This is your prime responsibility.

6 Decisions   People grow by making decisions and assuming responsibility. Make crystal clear what decision each manager is responsible for and what decisions you reserve for yourself. Have all the facts and counsel necessary—then decide and stick to it.

7 Criticism   Don't criticize people, but make a fair appraisal of their qualifications with their supervisor only (or someone assigned to do this). Remember, anything you say about someone may (and usually does) get back to them. There are few secrets.

8 See the good in people and try to develop those qualities.

9 Inefficiency   If it cannot be overcome, and an employee is obviously incapable of doing the job, either find a job he or she can do or terminate him or her now. Don't wait.

10 Manage your time; keep conversation short and to the point. Make every minute on the job count. Work fewer hours. Some of us waste half of our time.

11 Delegate and hold them accountable for the results.

12 Details   Let your staff take care of them. Save your energy for planning, thinking, working with department heads, promoting new ideas. Don't do anything someone else can do for you.

13 Ideas and competition   Ideas keep the business alive. Know what your competitors are doing and planning. Encourage all management to think about better ways of doing things and offer suggestions on anything that will improve business. Spend time and money on research and development.

14 Don't try to do an employee's job for him or her—counsel and make suggestions.

15 Think objectively and keep a sense of humour. Make the business fun for yourself and for others.

various meetings, whether they be weekly operations meetings, the monthly business meeting, the quarterly review, or the annual meeting. Managers need skills in leading creative meetings, negotiations, problem-solving groups, and various other situations where people meet to manage.

**One-hour meetings**  I do a great deal of counselling in meetings. I regularly call 'one-hour meetings' when I ask the team such basic questions as:

- 'How can we serve our customers better?'
- 'How can we become more efficient?'
- 'What makes a good marketing campaign?'
- 'How well do we work together?'

The ideas generated provide the basis for mutual counselling and help.

# Guidelines

Managerial counselling is about helping others to learn. It should be a reciprocal process where you help others and they help you.

What plans do you have to develop your managerial counselling skills in the next 12 months? The plan should focus on:

- the skills you need;
- the knowledge you need;
- the experience you need;
- the investment of time and money you will make;
- the outputs you will achieve.

If you have no plans you will learn mostly by accident—some good and some bad. If you have a plan you will be taking steps to reduce your risks—but you should also learn from the day-to-day hurly-burly of business. Keep a note of your learning points and counsel others as and when the opportunity arises.

# 12 Teamwork from the top please

*When all is said and done, there's more said than done.*

Lewis's Lament

## What is your impact?

It is commonly said that it is 'tough at the top'. I suspect this is true because many senior managers don't know what is going on. It is difficult to manage when you are flying blind.

Many managers are out of touch because they have not developed processes that enable them to get feedback on their own performance and on the performances of others. I shall concentrate here, particularly, on very senior managers at director and general manager level.

Sometimes they are their own worst enemies. Because they have reached senior rank, they surround themselves with various mechanisms that prevent them getting an accurate picture of what is going on. They may have the facts and figures, but often they do not have the feelings of the people. Consequently, they lose touch.

If top management are to improve their performance, it is essential that they have accurate and relevant feedback. In most organizations, the systems are such that financial information can be properly assessed. Increasingly, we are becoming more sophisticated in getting feedback from customers, although there is a considerable amount that needs to be done here to go beyond the standard market research questionnaire. The great weakness in my experience, however, is that top management do not get sufficient feedback from the people who report to them.

It is obvious why the weakness occurs. People are usually reluctant to give bad news to those who can control their destiny. Very often, however, the top managers do not get the good news either. People in our culture are often restricted in making praiseworthy comments in case it is felt that they are 'back-scratching' or 'toadying' to superiors.

There is a need, therefore, to find ways and means of helping top managers gain feedback, not just because it is a good thing but because it will help improve their own performance. How indeed can top managers learn to develop if they are not informed of where things are going right and where they are going wrong, particularly in so far as it affects their own managerial behaviour?

## Management by walking about

We have heard a great deal about 'management by walking about'. It is amazing to me that we have had to reinvent something so simple. It proves the danger of giving executives cars and offices in which they live their lives, locked away from the people who work in the organization.

I am, therefore, always impressed by executives who budget their time to meet staff on the production line, or at the office. Sir Hector Laing, when managing director of United Biscuits, told me he got to the office at 7.00 am to clear the paperwork and, providing there were no major meetings, he would, about mid-morning, drive or fly to one of the factories. He would drop in unannounced and talk to people, finding out what was important to them. While working as a consultant for the organization, I found this to be true and staff members acknowledged the importance of the CEO taking a personal interest.

Likewise, a chief executive of one of the largest banks in Australia told me that he regularly visits the branches and has discussions with the managers and staff. He said, however, that he found it difficult at times to persuade other senior managers to leave their central office desks and do likewise.

Getting out and about is a crucial aspect of a senior manager's job to get feedback from staff and customers. It needs to be done with discretion, so there are no quick-fire solutions undermining the local managers, or no suggestion of spying. If you are going to do a 'management by walking about', make it clear to everyone and also agree the rules up front.

# Top level team development

In my view the central task of all senior managers is developing effective teams. It is their distinctive contribution to the management development strategy of their organization. However, too many either ignore the challenge or do not know what it means. I do not say that lightly, for I have seen many senior managers cast a blind eye to the issue.

Indeed, I would have to say in a number of cases they have said one thing and then ignored their commitments. Taking time to talk through and give a lead to organization-wide team development is something that senior managers find difficult, unless there is some form of crisis—which then makes it the flavour of the month.

There are, of course, exceptions but look at your own organization and ask: Do the Board and executive directors devote sufficient time to developing excellent teams at all levels of the organization? Do they insist on a team appraisal review, such as that described in Chapter 3? Do they personally turn up to hear what teams are doing? Do they set up cross-functional and diagonal slice teams to learn and problem solve?

Let us look at some of the ways effective team development can be done. I, of course, declare an interest as I have been heavily involved in this area of management development and the examples cited are those where progress is definitely being made.

## The team development organization

The management development stage is an excellent vehicle for improving teamwork at all levels. It provides an organization which runs alongside the existing organization and enables people to speak freely. Let us, for example, call the day-to-day organization model A, which deals with operations. Let us, therefore, call the development organization, which is set up specifically to look at how we can improve matters, model B.

In my experience, model B should be conducted in an informal, relaxed atmosphere. There must also, however, be a structure and a timetable to plan it. It is best to set up opportunities where senior managers can meet with other colleagues at more junior levels in an off-site workshop environment. It is equally important that they meet for a specific purpose, preferably to consider new ways of doing things, or how to introduce new products or processes.

Wherever possible, I try to encourage top managers to meet in groups and work with people at other levels. In this way, they get to know each other as people rather than in their formal roles. It is important that such groups meet over a period of time and live in close proximity so that they can have opportunities for informal meetings at the bar and over meals.

In such a way one builds up a climate whereby comments and interactions can take place that would not occur in the normal workplace. Central, however, to the whole process, is the working together on joint tasks.

In this, the senior managers have to recognize that they have much to learn as well as much to give. Sometimes I ask them to be clients for groups who will report to them. This is useful but it still maintains the role distance between the higher level and the more junior levels.

## Mixed level teams

An effective way is to have tasks where different levels of people work together. Sometimes this can be done through simulation and case studies. Harvey-Jones, who was the chief executive of ICI and chairman for a number of years, indicates in his autobiography, *Making It Happen* (Harvey-Jones 1988), that one of the great learning experiences in his own career was working on a simulated management exercise with different levels.

They had an engineer, a finance person, and him, as a senior manager, plus a person who was a supervisor in the chemical company. They worked as a team to try to solve a problem but found that they were not making much progress. The engineer eventually walked out after his ideas had been rejected. The most junior member of the group, the supervisor, was working quietly on the problem and eventually came up with a solution.

They all learned much from the exercise, not the least of which was that they should listen to each other and not assume that the person who was the most senior should necessarily lead the group, or indeed have the most information. Harvey-Jones said it was indeed a humbling experience but one which, he said, guided much of his managerial behaviour from then on.

It is important, therefore, that we construct opportunities for top management to get feedback. I would even go so far as to suggest that, at least once a year, an off-site meeting should be called, where the top management work with other ranks to discuss how the company is being led. Basic questions, such as 'How do staff see the work of the senior managers?' or 'What would staff like senior managers to do in order to help improve their performance?' should be asked. Discussions like this are the basis of top management beginning to get some feedback on how they can begin to become more effective in developing effective teamwork and leadership.

## Team management preferences

My work with Dick McCann on team management has been central to the whole process. We have, through the creation of a software program, been able to provide managers with work preference profiles of how they see themselves and enable them to compare with other people. This technological tool has been valuable because it provides a vehicle as a basis for comparison. It, in effect, helps to facilitate discussions that might not otherwise take place. We now have many managers who ask for profiles so they can begin to share them with others and start a discussion on how to improve teamwork. This has also been done between levels and has provided a great opportunity to improve relationships.

Not all managers are keen to find out what other people think about them, or to learn from it. As we become more open to the challenges of business, however, it is important that managers do not press ahead without understanding the impact they are having upon others. If they do so, they may well be leaders without an army.

Any manager is only as good as the people who work for him or her. In order to keep on track, therefore, it is important that they have mechanisms to gain feedback. It is difficult to approach someone and ask 'How am I doing?'. It is much more preferable and productive if a proper process is set up, where open discussion can be facilitated towards some purpose.

It is for this reason that I have advocated the model B development organization, as something managers must put in place to run alongside the model A operations organization. This is an integral part of the management development process and senior managers need to look carefully at how they can set up a development organization in which they learn as much as everyone else.

Dick McCann and I, therefore, developed the *team management wheel* (Margerison and McCann 1990) based on the model shown in Figure 12.1, which outlines the major management roles that need to be played in any team. They range from providing information, generating ideas, representation, developing plans and systems, pushing for action and outputs through to detailed inspection work and maintaining values and standards. The model provides a simple may to show how managers can assess their teams.

Managers say it is particularly helpful to get a personal profile of over 4,000 words, based on the *team management index*, on how they see their preferred way of working, which they can use to share and compare with other team members. These profiles provide the basis for giving and gaining feedback on how people see themselves and what they do. That is one way to facilitate managerial feedback.

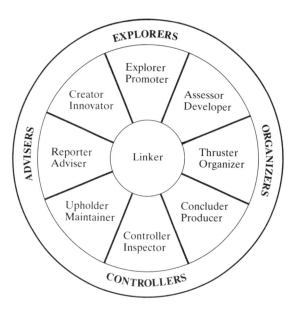

**Figure 12.1**   *The Margerison–McCann team management wheel*

# Managerial linkers

We have found that successful managers need to be effective linkers. This involves two major activities: internal linking and external linking. Some managers do one or the other well, but the all-round manager does both.

- *Internal linking* is the work done with your own team to help them to work together effectively. In particular it involves working with each person's work preferences and helping that person to contribute fully to the team.
- *External linking* involves representing the team in various ways within the organization. This may involve gaining more resources or putting forward a proposal on behalf of the group. Equally, it means linking the policies and plans set by the Board to your team and gaining their support.

The question of how you can identify an effective managerial linker has been asked many times. We have found no universal pen and paper test that will tell us, but we have found a straightforward human test. The answer is to ask the team members.

They invariably know whether their manager is being an effective linker or not. They have to work with him or her each day and know whether they are being kept up to date and whether their interests are being represented. In our work on team management we have identified examples and illustrations of what effective linkers do. These show the linkers are not only effective at the traditional tasks of planning, organizing and controlling but are also adept at organizational politics and are particularly effective in persuading colleagues at the same level or higher in the organization.

To test your linking skills, therefore, why not call your group together and ask them to state the key linking activities that they feel are important within the team and outside the team, upwards and laterally. Then ask them to advise you on ways things can be improved. It is a team development effort that may produce a few surprises.

## How team management works

The Margerison–McCann team management approach is used by major companies to improve performance. Some of the notable applications are:

- HEWLETT PACKARD have involved over 2,000 of their managers in team management development. Considerable work has been done with their computer sales teams. They spend two days away, looking at how they operate as a team. Day 1 involves looking at the theory of team management and the roles. During this time, they receive their own personal profiles and share these. Day 2 is where the manager of the team takes the lead in discussing with his or her colleagues how they will improve performance and, in the context of the team management wheel, where they will strengthen their efforts.

- AUSTRALIAN AIRLINES have used the team management approach to improve teamwork in the cockpit between captains and crew. This involved all 600 aircrew in a programme to look at the way interpersonal factors influenced effective flight management.

- ARTHUR ANDERSEN, the accounting partnership, have used team management on their internal development programmes. Increasingly, accountants and auditors need to work as a team and the management development of their professions includes an understanding of how work preferences influence behaviour.

- THE BRITISH TRAINING AGENCY is the largest training organization in the UK and responsible, among other activities, for designing training programmes for various government departments. It uses team management systems to guide managers and staff on how to develop improved work relationships.

- THE HONG KONG BANK have also adopted the team management systems approach to improving the way in which branch managers and their teams work.

The message is that management development is a team development effort as well as an individual activity, and one without the other is not sufficient.

## As CEO, what will you do?

I believe that management development is only limited by the creativity of those involved, yet on only a few occasions can I remember any of my own managers, or others I have known, calling their team together and having a meeting purely and simply on ideas for improving management development. Let us, therefore, sit in on how one of these wild ideas meetings could go. The following transcript is my view of what a Board of Directors might say if they really got switched on to management development.

CEO (*chief executive*): Today we have the opportunity to put forward any ideas that we feel will be of benefit to our company, providing it means we spend money on developing our people rather than investing in machinery. Every idea is welcome no matter how wild. We shall keep a list of all of them and implement as many as we can.

FD (*finance director*): Let's start with the life blood of our company and talk about money. I bet if we were to test our staff, very few would know how much is invested and where the money is spent. I would like to see every member of staff right down to the guy on the front gate involved in at least one project to assess the cost of the work they do and its benefit to the company. They would also come up with recommendations on what they can do to improve the return on the time they spend at work.

PD (*production director*): That's OK for certain jobs but not for those who are involved, say, in research or security. However, all our staff should be able to measure their productivity in some way and I propose that we ask them to do it and tell us what they have learned.

MD (*marketing director*): Both of these are interesting ideas but people find it very difficult to be self-critical. I suggest that we get people from different functions to meet and assess each other's jobs. This would be an annual audit but between people who don't normally work together.

HRD (*human resources director*): To me the most important thing we should do is ensure that every one of the staff meet at least one customer during the year and listens to what that customer has to say.

CEO: It's interesting that so far we have talked about staff in general. What do you feel we should encourage managers to do as the rest of the staff take their lead from them?

MD: Our managers are far too removed from the thinking on the shopfloor. We should set an example and make ourselves available to run a shift with the foreman and go out on deliveries with our truck drivers. We should only go by invitation but we should make it clear that we are there to learn and not to interfere with operations.

PD: I know that we would be appreciated by some of the staff while others would regard it as spying. I believe it would have to be a two-way street and shopfloor people should be given access to the Boardroom and the meetings we attend.

HRD: We are getting into the corridor of power issues now. How open can we be? I favour a representative democracy in the organization that runs alongside the executive system where anyone can be elected on a 'one-person one-vote' basis to draw up rules about how we should manage the organization and this would cover everything from workers' rights through to car parking regulations. This would get everyone thinking about management issues and how to influence change.

CEO: I want everyone involved in the management of change and that to me is the cornerstone on which we should build our management development strategy. Each year every person should be involved in a change project outside their normal area of expertise. They should act as consultants but concentrate on getting people to think through and diagnose problems and opportunities rather than providing solutions. Then everyone might learn, particularly if we insist that they have to write up their findings and present them to their clients.

MD: I agree but I would also start that nearer home and ask all managers to write down what they have learned in the last 12 months and to share this information with others at special workshops so we all gain the benefit of each other's experience.

CEO: We've had some interesting ideas but how radical are they?

HRD: I'm keen on this self-appraisal approach and I propose that managers are never given a pay rise until they conduct all their performance review interviews and have them signed off as satisfactory. Also I propose that managers are not eligible for promotion until they convince us that they have developed a worthy successor.

PD: We have got to give more people profit and loss responsibility. That is the only way we shall find out if they can run a business. Therefore let us buy some small units where we can give some of our up-and-coming managers a chance to sharpen their wits.

MD: The real skill is in picking and managing the right people. Too many of our managers do not get a chance to do this until they are well into their thirties. I propose these smaller units be given over to managers between the ages of 25 and 30 so they have an opportunity to show what they can do.

HRD: That is a good idea providing it's not sink or swim. We've got quite a lot of retired managers who would welcome the opportunity to be an unofficial chairman and mentor to these younger managers.

PD: Management is about teamwork. The manager is the captain of his or her team. I want to see the managers getting their teams together and asking them how they, as managers, are performing. Until the captain is told by the players how to improve his or her own game, the captain will not have the necessary feedback to change and improve.

MD: We've talked little about skills and I believe that feedback skills are crucial to any manager's success—both how to give and how to receive. I favour some reverse role-plays where managers not only play customers but role-play their own staff on difficult issues and the staff take the role of the manager.

CEO: Let's conclude this session by taking all the ideas away and thinking about them. I would just add one more and that is that we as directors should start off the new approach to management development by conducting an audit of each other's jobs and how we do them, particularly in terms of the service we give each other. Then we should set an example to everyone by making presentations on how we are trying to improve teamwork at the top. Maybe a bit of leadership here will be helpful.

If you were the management development manager, what would you do next?

# Team meetings

Team management can be improved in various ways. A start is to audit the weekly, monthly and quarterly meetings. Do you have them and how effective are they? If in doubt, ask everyone at the next meeting. If you are serious about it, do not have any item on the agenda other than: 'What does teamwork mean to us and how can we improve it?'

Beyond this level, there needs to be a strategy for improving teamwork in the organization and this must come from the top. Once everyone knows that the senior managers are keen to develop improved cooperation within and between teams, the results will come in the form of greater linking, improved motivation, increased productivity and a more integrated approach.

## Guidelines

To what extent do you gather feedback from your team and get them to share with each other how to improve performance?

What roles do you play well and which do you need to improve?

There are many ways of improving teamwork and team management but the example must be given from the top.

The emphasis should not be on more meetings or workshops but on improving the quality of the current gatherings. This means looking at how they are conducted rather than what is discussed.

At your next team meeting, why not have only one topic on the agenda: 'Our team—how well do we work together and what can we do to improve our own performance and our performance with other parts of the organization?' This will be a challenging event and everyone should learn something of importance, particularly you.

# 13 Management education and the rise of the corporate business school

*All you need in life is ignorance and confidence and then success is sure.*

Mark Twain

## Linking work to development

I was discussing management development with the main Board Director of a large chemical company. He said, 'We find it difficult to send more than one or two people a year to business schools. Firstly, it takes far too much time for people who are in mid-career to be away from their jobs, for such a period of time. In addition, the cost of the programmes, plus the salary bill that we have to pay, is too high. Furthermore, we have got no guarantee that they will stay with us when they return.'

We discussed the importance of developing managers who are excellent technical specialists to widen their skills and, at the same time, continue to do a good job for the company. I suggested that we design a company business school programme, where we would bring the faculty to the company instead of the managers leaving to go to university. This idea started a major association between me, other colleagues and the company, through which we developed the equivalent of a Master of Business Administration degree for a number of the organization's high fliers using the action learning approach.

For a period of 18 months the company allowed 15 managers to have one day a fortnight in which to attend workshops, on a wide range of management subjects, dealing with finance, marketing, human resources, operations and strategy. In addition, there were various weekend sessions on key topics, such as international business, communications, information management and team management. Throughout the whole programme, the managers had to translate the ideas that were being developed into action, through real projects. These projects were nominated by senior managers in the organization and the participants were tutored on how, for example, to launch new products, assess the potential of new technology, make an assessment of capital expenditure and also deal with less tangible items such as improving the industrial relations climate and working out ways and means for improving communication.

## Joint development activities

One of the earliest and most interesting examples of this approach to management education and development was initiated by John Morris (1982) when he was a professor at the Manchester Business School. He started the first JDA programme in conjunction with Rolls Royce in

1969 and has subsequently worked with major companies in many countries applying the principles, which are:

- that there should be work projects as the centre of doing and learning;
- that the projects should be chosen by senior management, who should follow through and support those who are assigned to those projects;
- that there should be an association with an academic or consultancy organization who provide guidance on new skills and methods.

There are similarities between JDAs, as Morris calls them, and action learning as they both rely on real work as the centre of the learning process.

Throughout the programme we did with the chemical company, the participants had to write up what they did and to describe, explain and prescribe, as a result of their analysis. They also had to present their ideas to other colleagues and senior managers and indicate not only what they intended to do, but what they had actually achieved. The programme was a great success and provided the basis for considering the extension of the business school concept to other levels within the organization.

## Hamburger University and others

Indeed, a number of organizations have already brought in their own business schools to facilitate the development of their managers. One of the earliest of these was the McDonald Hamburger chain. They founded, much to the amusement of many, Hamburger University. While it was regarded as a joke by some sceptics, the McDonald organization was ahead of its time. They recognized that the way to improve their effectiveness was to invest in their people and help them learn about their own business by studying it in some depth, through real case studies related to McDonald operations.

Other organizations, such as the Disney Corporation, the GE Company in the USA and the GEC in the UK have all shown how the corporate business school can work to improve managerial and organizational performance. I find it surprising that so few other organizations have taken this option seriously. While most of them set up specialized resources in research and development and have vast expenditure on laboratories, they do not seem willing to spend even a fraction of that money on developing their people through a company business school.

While these organizations will put literally millions of dollars into advertising—much of it totally wasted—they seem unwilling to invest in developing their people, who could do a far better job of directing the company towards the sales targets that they are pursuing through advertising, if only they were equipped with the knowledge and skills to do so.

It is an indictment of so many organizations that they ignore the value of setting up their own business school in favour of sending people to short courses elsewhere. Those people then have the major problem of transferring any knowledge they receive back into a culture that is not ready to receive it because people have not shared the experience.

The great value of the corporate business school is that it allows staff from the same organization to consider ways and means of working together more effectively to improve performance, and to raise productivity and profits through a better service to customers. This, in my view, is infinitely better than sending individuals hither and yon in search of the touchstone of wisdom, which is usually within the organization.

This is not to deny the value of searching for ideas from other people or from other organizations. First things must come first, however, and the establishment of a company business school is a relatively small investment for most organizations in terms of the returns that can be gained through motivation, morale, plus the real enhancement of performance from the sharing and comparing of experience.

## MBA company/ university joint ventures

Until recently, all MBA education was conducted off site in business schools. As Hussey (1990) indicates in his UK study, this is rapidly changing. In 1988 there were only about 200 students registered in a company-related MBA programme. In the succeeding two years this was estimated to have grown to 400. It is further estimated that up to one-third of British MBA students will be studying via this route within a short period of time.

This will be encouraged by the Ashridge and City University link up, the executive MBA such as that at Cranfield, and the Warwick and Open University distance learning MBA. It seems that, in this respect, the UK may be ahead of the USA in some areas.

Increasingly, the UK universities are having to raise more and more of their own revenue. The drive towards joint ventures with industry and commerce is, therefore, not all educational enlightenment. The cold winds of debt are striking at the coffers and management education is one area where educators can raise revenue.

The important point is that the educational methods will now have to become customer orientated, with all those good lecture notes put to good use in practice. It will be interesting to see how many can practise what they preach. I have mentioned my association with the International Management Centres as one practical example of how the joint venture approach can work effectively using the action learning approach.

A number of major organizations, such as DuPont, The Grand Metropolitan Hotels, International Distillers and Vintners, Ernst Young the Accountants, ICI, Allied Irish Banks, Seagrams, and various others, have taken advantage of their strategic initiative. In the process, they have been able to develop their people at relatively low cost, and in so doing have tackled major business issues that have more than paid for the programmes.

It is this kind of innovative thinking that must become more prevalent in the 1990s. It will only happen if senior managers begin to realize that management development is the key that unlocks the door to improved performance. In doing so they will provide a dynamic structure that will enable people to achieve their potential. This, in my view, is one of the key factors that will differentiate the successful from the unsuccessful organizations as we move towards the year 2000.

**The Westpac Bank case**

Westpac is one of Australia's largest banks, employing nearly 50 000 people. In1987 it decided to take training so seriously that it set up its own company called Westpac Training Services to provide services to its own staff on a fee-paying basis.

According to Jim Huey (1989), the then executive director, 'Eight per cent of our payroll is already spent on training.' He estimated that direct expenditure on training was close to 50 million Australian dollars. The survival of the training company is now based on the service it provides. To do this, Huey stressed, 'we have made it clear that strategies to be developed must be linked to overall human resources strategies, which in turn, must be linked to our corporate objectives'.

Westpac has gone so far as to set up its own Management Training Institute. This organization has to survive on its merits by providing programmes of relevance to the managers of the bank who have a choice of going elsewhere for such services.

Westpac Training Services provide a total range of training, from customer services at the local branch where you deposit or withdraw cash, through to advanced management training. Further, they have decentralized the provision of the training to regional groups, who serve managers in their area. In all, over 300 people are employed in the training company, with 40 of them training design and development work.

In Westpac, the line managers are the customers and clients. Those managers hold the training budget for people in their area. That money can be spent on the company business school, or on outside programmes. Managers have a choice. Westpac Training Services has to compete for the custom and survive like any business on the sales it makes. This practical approach to the strategy and structure of training and management development is one we shall see more of in the 1990s.

**British and American Tobacco Industries**

The importance of integrating 'on-the-job' management development with 'off-the-job' development is recognized in the design of a programme constructed by Jim Butler (1990) and his colleagues at BAT Industries. Instead of the conventional 'this will be good for you' design, they decided to build it around company strategies and projects.

Prior to the programme, all participants gain a briefing in their own organizational surroundings. About a month later, they attend a six-day programme at the Chelwood Vatchery Company College. Teams are formed to work on key issues. This provides the base upon which the applied work is then done. At the end of the period, the teams return to Chelwood for a sharing, comparing and learning session. Projects have involved looking at the change of a management structure; customers services operations; information technology strategy and various other initiatives. This again shows the importance of a design that combines theory with practice and reflection and action with a follow through to the sharing of results.

**The Scandinavian consortium**

One of the most interesting cooperative management development initiatives is that between the four Nordic Management Development Institutes from Sweden, Norway, Finland, and Denmark. They have joined together to provide an action learning-based management programme, with eight major companies involved.

Participants work in groups of four on real projects put forward by their organizations. The group members come from different countries. participants are encouraged to establish similar groups in their own organizations, involving their manager, subordinates, and colleagues. The programme lasts for almost 12 months, and 40 days are allocated for 'off-the-job' aspects, of which about half are for seminars and half are for action applications.

**University education or training**

The University of Ulster has developed an action MBA which includes a great deal of involvement on real projects with local companies. There are 12 months of conventional classroom study, plus an overseas assignment followed by six months of in-company project work.

Increasingly, other universities are getting the message that it is not just what you know but what you do that is important. This is a far cry from my own eduction at tertiary level when I spent three years at the London School of Economics studying for an economics degree. I cannot ever recollect being asked once to go into the city of London and test any of the theories or report back on what people were actually doing to make the economy work. A study of taxi drivers, or the management of a fish and chip shop, would certainly have taught my colleagues and me many lessons. It may have led us to challenge the conventional wisdom and perhaps that is why we were never encouraged to study the real world.

Management education today has to be practical and relevant. If you cannot use it, why learn it? That may not be applicable to all tertiary programmes but should be applicable to management development courses.

**Leadership at General Foods**

In his book, *Executive Development*, Jim Bolt (1989) provides examples of how America's largest companies are taking management development seriously. They may not all claim to have their own business school, but that is what they are in effect doing.

General Foods recognized the need to improve performance and chose to do so using management development as a major way to achieve business objectives. Managers, therefore, were involved in a programme that focused on how to:

- identify what can be achieved;
- identify the ways change could be introduced;
- recognize, via feedback from staff, the impact the manager has as a leader;

- recognize strategies for empowering his or her group;
- identify personal actions that reinforce and reward values and behaviours needed to achieve goals.

This was the beginning of a wide-ranging, successful change programme.

## What makes the difference?

From his study of large, medium and small corporations, Bolt reaches similar conclusions to my own observations which, simply stated, are:

- senior management must be involved from the start;
- steering committees, involving key political players, are a key to acceptability;
- sound research on the needs is never wasted if you involve the managers in this process;
- programme design must relate to the needs and again involve managers in testing and development;
- the implementation must be top class and relevant to real work;
- the faculty and advisers must be top supportive people, able to facilitate on real world problems and opportunities;
- the learning approach should be participative and based on learning by doing, supplemented by information sessions;
- emphasis must be placed on getting results and transferring the learning to the job.

## Is management education a hoax?

My colleague, Dr Jim Kable (1988), caused a storm when he suggested that a great deal of management education was a hoax. He has had a great deal of experience in conducting management programmes and was concerned that many of the people who attended did so for the wrong reasons. He cited the lady who turned up because, on the morning of the programme, the original nominee could not make it, so she was asked to stand in. She did not know how the course would benefit her but she turned up. He cites many other examples of people being sent to be 'reformed' in two days. They are sent with no briefing or any training needs assessment. It also applies at the MBA level, where people turn up to get the paper qualification rather than the education.

We have all experienced similar cases. The answer lies in planning and consultation. It seems obvious that before people attend a management course they should write down what they want to achieve, and when they return they should write down what they have gained and how they will apply it. Normally, the only assessment made, is on the course. The assessment should be by the participants on themselves—what was learned and what action will be taken. This should form the basis of the discussion with their manager.

We shall then have a situation where managerial education is taken seriously, as it is in a number of organizations who apply such a disciplined approach to courses. After all, management education is only a part of management development and needs to be integrated into the total system.

# Are MBAs worth while?

The Master of Business Administration degree has become the most popular postgraduate qualification at universities. In the USA, it is estimated that at any one time there are over 250 000 people studying for an MBA degree. In Europe, the number is much smaller but growing rapidly. But in Japan and West Germany, two of the leading nations economically, the MBA is not a major university degree.

Much controversy surrounds the MBA degree. Various studies have been made which allege that the investment in the MBA degree may pay off for the individual participant but that there is little evidence of how such education has increased the value of the business corporations. Many companies are now sceptical of MBA graduates, who want high salaries but do not seem to have the managerial skills to go with their knowledge.

My view, however, is that MBAs are worth while, providing the following points are built in to the decision to participate:

- You should be at least 26 years of age.
- You should have completed an undergraduate degree or similar professional qualification.
- You should have at least three years of work experience, preferably in an organizational team.
- You should have a strong desire to manage, whether it be as an executive or as a consultant.
- You should be prepared to do the MBA on a part-time basis using real projects from work as case studies for applying your learning.
- You should be prepared to work at the MBA in groups rather than as an individual activity, as managing is a group-based task.
- You should enter into contracts with yourself and your manager and colleagues to practice regularly what you learn and show what you have done.

Overall, I favour the corporate business school approach. This, increasingly, will not be an all in-house affair. It will be a joint venture arrangement between an employer and a business school. I have mentioned the action learning MBA that was designed for ICI Australia, who had a joint venture with the International Management Centre. Many others are now developing and I believe the way ahead lies in the link between business and educational organizations.

# How adults learn

Malcolm Knowles (1980)—who for many years was a director of the YMCA in the USA and later Professor of Education at Boston University—has also pressed hard to develop ways and means of facilitating personal development within the organization, rather than just in the classroom.

He has focused particularly on the adult learner who, he feels, is a neglected species. He confronts the old model whereby a person once trained is set up for life. Today we need to train and retrain regularly to keep up to date. Knowles therefore emphasizes we must place more attention on andragogy—the process by which we learn—rather than just pedagogy, which emphasizes how we are taught.

He has worked with major corporations and government agencies to design programmes based on the principles that concentrate on learning from experience, project-orientated development, self-awareness and organizing learning around real activities. In particular, he has indicated the need for a learning contract whereby objectives and schedules are agreed and planned action then takes place.

So what learning contract will you establish for the next six months to one year? You can take responsibility for your own learning by writing a contract with yourself to invest time, energy and money in development activities. You can later measure how effective you were. So what are your learning objectives and methods for the next year?

## What should a manager know?

This is a question every manager should ask himself, or herself, on a regular basis. I have found it helpful to distinguish between internal and external requirements. Internal issues relate to the company and how it works. External issues relate to subjects and matters outside the organization. Table 13.1 provides a checklist that includes subjects in which every manager should have a basic understanding. The areas given are those I keep in my mind. Add your own, then identify what you will do in each area this year to improve your management development.

**Table 13.1**   *Checklist of managerial requirements*

|    | Internal | External | Subjects |
|----|----------|----------|----------|
| 1  | Mission | Customers | Finance |
| 2  | Strategy | Competitors | Marketing |
| 3  | Product | Suppliers | Law |
| 4  | Staff | Economy | Human resources |
| 5  | Prices | Professions | Operations management |
| 6  | Politics | Political trends | Information management |
| 7  | Systems | Market trends | Statistical analysis |
| 8  | Plans | Environmental issues | Economics |
| 9  | Budgets | Unions | Accounting |
| 10 | Organization | International issues | Personal computing skills |

## Guidelines

More and more organizations will start their own business schools, establish their own faculty (usually on a temporary, as required, basis) and integrate work and learning. It is an exciting prospect when managers, like apprentices throughout time, regard the place of work as their best training ground.

The corporate business school will indeed become a major driving force for innovation, product development, profitability, quality, efficiency and effectiveness, not because it teaches but because managers can, under its umbrella, meet and learn from each other. What do you need to do in order to foster an in-company business school? With whom will you consult?

What is your own educational contract? Development must start with you, so set down what you intend to learn and then let others know. That in itself is the basis of a learning contract. In so doing, you will encourage others to do likewise and also probably gain a great deal of help from them once people know what you are trying to achieve.

# 14 The politics of management development

## Making plans work

Sir Michael Edwards, who took on the arduous job of reforming the British Leyland car-making giant, said, 'Our task as leaders is to encourage change to take place in a constructive way, preferably by evolution rather than revolution. When people over the years have not faced up to change, whole companies, whole industries, and indeed, whole empires and civilizations have disappeared. Change is inevitable. This force should be recognized and diverted to the common good rather than resisted in a totally negative way.'

It is for such reasons that I regard planning as a priority for managers. We are primarily paid not just to manage today's business but to anticipate tomorrow's and ensure that we are ready to meet the challenges. This, therefore, is a key aspect of management development.

Another great leader, Dwight Eisenhower, who was the Commander of the Allied Forces during the Second World War and later became President of the United States, said that 'Plans may be nothing, but planning is everything.' It is the active process of thinking things through that is crucial to giving the direction in which everyone needs to put their energy if success is to be achieved.

How, therefore, can we improve our planning processes? Many companies are now well organized in terms of setting mission statements, developing objectives, defining strategies, preparing budgets and allocating roles and deadlines. That, after all, is what all the good textbooks say should be done. The problem, in my experience, is that plans are made but very few of the people in an organization understand them.

The people are not unintelligent, or indeed even uninterested. The simple fact is that senior managers have not involved their staff and colleagues at other levels in the planning process. The politics of management development are, therefore, central to any planning for change.

Japanese companies, because of their economic success, are frequently cited as examples from which we should learn. This may or may not depend upon various cultural differences. There is, however, one outstanding way in which they show the way forward and that is the commitment they have to involve people from various levels in the planning process. The Ringi system and the process of Nemawashi provide two concepts for involving people in thinking through the future. The result: people not only know what is happening but have a contribution to make in the process.

Too often, planning in the western organizations is seen as a secret activity. Corporate plans are devised by a few select individuals in locked rooms. The creation of corporate planning departments has made the task a profession in its own right. Indeed, at present, when takeovers are an integral part of business life, one can understand this mentality. However, such secrecy undermines management development.

## Political planning levels

In order to run a business in which you have the commitment of the people, it is vital that they are involved in plans that affect their operations. Therefore, each year a major part of management development should be to encourage people, at all levels, to plan their own destiny, and this should reflect around a number of levels:

1 *Individual development plan*   Yourself: what do you plan to do in order to extend your own personal skills and competencies during the year?
2 *Job improvement plan*   Your job: what plans do you have to improve your performance and the way in which your job is done?
3 *Team improvement plan*   Your team: what plans do you have for their contribution to the team and the overall way in which the team can improve its performance?
4 *Division plan*   Your division: what plans do you have that can begin to influence the wider operations, within which their own team works?
5 *Organization plan*   Your organization: what plans and ideas do you have that can make a contribution to the total organization?

All of these levels are crucial. The Toyota organization proves it. Each individual can make a major contribution to the organization as a whole. They show through their suggestions scheme that if the conditions are right, people can be involved in putting forward ideas that will influence the planning process. It is not, however, just a suggestion box that is required. It is the involvement of people in thinking through the ideas, in terms of what they mean in practice.

This is the challenge for management development. To meet this challenge, we must set up ways and means in which people have time to think, to meet and to discuss the issues in a positive, pro-active way. Senior management must find time to be interested in these ideas and give positive feedback.

In this way, management development will aid the planning process and, in return, people will become more effective because they know what is going on and have shared in the creation of the future. They will then be committed to implementing the plans that eventually emerge.

## Money and management development

Management development is now a substantial business. I was recently presented with a government paper asking me to submit a proposal for a programme that will involve the expenditure of over $115 million during a three-year period. Now this may sound a great deal of money. It has to be spent, however, on 40 000 managers.

So what advice would you give? The managers in question are all aged between 35 and 45 and 60 per cent of them work in regional offices. Half of those working at the central offices and three-quarters of those working in the regions have little chance of further promotion given the limited vacancies.

Last year 80 per cent of the managers had no training and there is a recognized need to develop skills in human resource management, information systems and performance appraisal programmes.

In my view, the formal off-the-job programme, however designed, can never do justice to such a large cadre of managers. Even if you have 20 people on each course, it will mean 2 000 courses which, if they last five days, means 10 000 training days.

We, therefore, have to think of a more lateral and cost-effective way to develop managers. My view is that it can only be done if managers take responsibility for developing each other and each person takes self-development as a major priority.

Therefore, establishing a group of managers who are shown how to conduct effective action learning initiatives is one vital way to proceed. They should then be charged with the vital task of developing their team members in a planned and systematic way. Each manager therefore becomes a management development manager. Only in this way can we hope to deal with large-scale programmes of this kind.

Alongside the managerial initiatives, there must be a well-organized support system that provides advice on resources, access to particular information and consultancy guidance. The accountability for management development, however, must be with the managers. It is one task they cannot delegate.

## Political aspects

Management development is a political activity. It involves decisions on people's careers and livelihood. It involves decisions on who should get which jobs. Such actions inevitably decide who has influence and power and also who gets paid more than someone else. The politics of management development should, therefore, not be underestimated. To ensure that there are clear policies and processes, it is vital that the senior management team agree the principles upon which issues—such as internal versus external appointments, the criteria for promotion, the basis upon which people will be rewarded and the provision of executive development opportunities—will be provided.

In too many organizations there is little formally written down about these aspects of policy. It is only when an organization begins to look seriously at the contracts it has with managers that the importance of such policies become obvious. In a recent assignment, I was asked to recommend to a large organization how it should develop management development policies, consistent with the move towards fixed-term contracts.

This has two important aspects. First, the organization wanted to say something meaningful to its managers and new recruits about what they could expect from the organization, in terms of being developed to fulfil the job demands that they were given. Reciprocally, they wanted a policy that committed the managers to taking their own development seriously and, in particular, developing members of their team.

As one senior manager said, 'It is important, if we are going to hold people to account on contracts, that we spell out clearly what is required. It is no use in two or three years' time trying to hold people back from promotion, or even dismissing them, for not performing well in developing others, or themselves, when there was no obligation in the first instance to do so.'

I have worked closely, therefore, with this organization, and others, to develop clear and concise management development policies. Typically, I set up a steering committee of senior managers, who provide the key political contacts to ensure we are on track. The vitally important issue, therefore, is to consult with all managers who will be involved.

I normally, therefore, have a meeting with the steering committee and we talk through the terms of reference. This is usually set by the chief executive and others, in the context of the business objectives. The terms of reference often refer to values, style of management, the need for more cooperation and other issues, which would help improve organizational performance.

## The political levels of action

Management development, therefore, needs to be democratic. It is not just a question of putting on an executive programme. It is also not just a matter of introducing a performance review system, or a good compensation package. It means involving managers and assessing what management development means to them and how they can diagnose the problems that they feel should be addressed. Then they can develop options and alternatives to cope with those issues.

This is what I mean by the politics of management development. Managers are reluctant to commit themselves to activities in which they have not themselves been consulted or involved. Senior managers wish to recognize that staff at all levels need to have a say in their own future. Structures and forums for this to happen, therefore, need to be established. It is not just a matter of management and union negotiators coming to an agreement. The politics of management development need to be reflected at every level, from individual plans, performance reviews, team development, promotion committees and salary and compensation reviews.

One way to do this is to open up these areas for an audit by groups of managers who currently do not have positions of influence or authority in those areas. Let them assess how effective and fair the systems are and then report publicly on their findings. That is a political process of *Glasnost* from which many organizations would benefit. The resulting *Perestroika* would, no doubt, improve motivation and opportunity.

I have been involved in such management development. The participants learn an enormous amount about parts of the business that previously were a mystery. In addition, the results emerging sharpen the management development system and keep all involved with it honest and on their toes. It is about time that management development managers took their own medicine and invited line managers to study the way they do their job.

**A case example**  The company employs about 20 000 people in a wide variety of businesses ranging from glass and plastic bottle manufacture, through to computer technology applications. I was asked by the directors to give advice on the management development policies and practices.

I asked the Executive Board to identify what they felt was good and bad about the existing approach in the company. They concluded that in a number of areas a great deal needed to be improved. I suggested they choose three teams of people to assess the important areas and test their assumptions. Over a period of three months these teams, each with seven members drawn from the top 400 managers, were given guidance on how to audit management development.

One group surveyed the top 400 managers. The next group surveyed those who reported to the top 400 and the third group studied how 13 other companies organized management development. Their face-to-face feedback to the Board was a no-nonsense assessment of what they found and the action proposed. The Executive Board recognized the truth of what they were saying and voted immediately for a major investment in management development.

This is an example of the positive aspects of management development politics at work. The Board had the courage to allow senior managers to investigate and the managers had the courage to tell it as they saw it. The result was resources were allocated to a cause for concern where the motivation level to act had been raised to a high level through political participation.

**The hard and soft aspects of change**  In my experience, one of the most vital areas for management development is in the processes of how to get things done. While managers can learn how to read a balance sheet, or write a marketing plan, or understand the principle of quality control, the really difficult task is doing something useful with the knowledge and techniques.

Those managers who can manage the process of getting people together to make things work, are those who are really managing. That is why many MBA graduates are not respected in industry. They may know a great deal about techniques and principles but they have not acquired the skills of how to get the commitment and support of others. It may be that the 'streetwise' manager, who is not formally qualified, can do this well, even though he or she may not have taken formal courses.

What do these managers who ensure action is taken do, and can we develop their skills? If you ask people they will use general phrases such as, 'they are good communicators', but that does not tell us what they do. Most of them have political processes at work influencing management development. I have observed what effective managers do and the following examples give some key indicators. On the surface, the points might look easy but, like most skills, they develop with practise. These people are managers who have developed good linking skills.

**Linking skills examples**

'I have breakfast meetings,' said one manager in a computer sales business. 'Once a month I get the 30 people in my team together. Before the meeting I ask a few people to be prepared to say what they have done that has worked in the last month and indicate the results. It is a great way to share success and motivate people. It's one of the best things I've done. It keeps me in touch with the sales reps and it keeps them in touch with each other.'

'I have one-hour meetings on specific issues', said another manager. 'I agree with the team what these are and ask one person to lead a discussion. That person has to produce a statement of the issue on one page. Our job is to come up with options for action. At the end of the meeting the person who leads it has to write up a note of understanding and circulate it to the others. I find we really achieve much in the hour. It concentrates everyone's attention and helps in the mutual sharing and solving of problems.'

'I have a walk around and ask lots of questions', said another. 'If people tell me bad news, as they often do, I try not to give an instant judgement. I take the information away and call a meeting so that those accountable can take action.'

'Besides the task-orientated meetings where we discuss hard stuff like budgets, production targets, sales reports and so on, I also run meetings on the soft stuff. I choose a topic in which everyone is interested and get the team together to discuss things like "How much job satisfaction do we have here and how could it be improved?", "What do we do well and what do we do badly and what should we do about both?", "What creative ideas do we have for how we can work better as a team?", "What should we assess, examine and study, in order to improve the way we work?".'

These are all examples of what, in my view, effective linkers in team management do. They concentrate as much on the process as on the content of management. This is the area in which we need to spend more time developing managerial competence. In the end, it is these skills and behaviours that will encourage management development at all levels.

# International politics and management development

As we enter the 1990s, we are seeing some extraordinary political changes in Europe, which will have major implications for management development. The moves in Hungary, Poland and Yugoslavia, among others, towards a more market-orientated economy will place considerable demands on the managerial skills and abilities of executives at all levels.

It will not be easy to move from a centrally planned system where prices have been artificially fixed to a system where organizations have to survive on their own merits. The key to the successful transfer will be the small 'p' politics of management development.

The skills and abilities developed in western countries can be of enormous benefit if adapted to the local requirements and this may best be facilitated not by gratuitous advice but by joint ventures. Let us examine one particular case that has been well documented and also review some trends in the UK and Japan.

**Management in Russia**

I was fascinated when reading the book *Perestroika* by the President of the Soviet Union, Mikhail Gorbachev (1987), to see the importance he places on management development. He describes how the 280 million people that comprise the Soviet Union have fallen on hard times because of, among other things, inadequate management. His book should be read by all managers, for it is an example that others should follow in diagnosing the issues. These are some of his outspoken comments about the nation he leads.

With us the consumer found himself totally at the mercy of the producer and had to make do with what the latter chose to give him.

Parasitical attitudes were on the rise, the prestige of conscientious and high quality labor began to diminish and a 'wage levelling' mentality was becoming widespread.

An absurd situation was developing. The Soviet Union, the world's biggest producer of steel, raw materials, fuel and energy, has shortfalls in them due to wasteful or inefficient use.

Everyone started noticing the stagnation among the leadership and the violation of the national processes of change there.

Fewer and fewer demands were made on discipline and responsibility.

Many party members in leading posts stood beyond control and criticism, which led to failures in work and to serious malpractices.

It is against this background that Gorbachev persuaded the April 1985 Plenary meeting of the Central Committee to adopt his restructuring strategy which he called *perestroika*. This, he says, 'concerns virtually every main aspect of public life'. He defines it as covering a more democratic approach, which should include, 'increased independence of enterprises and associations, their transition to full self-accounting and self-financing and granting all appropriate rights to work collectives. They will now be fully responsible for efficient management and end results.'

Now, if all this is to come about, it will require probably the largest management development programme the world has ever seen. Managers who previously have only had to produce what the central plan told them will now have to identify what is required and find and manage the resources to achieve the goals. How different will this be from management development in the USA, or the UK, or Australia?

I am certain that, despite the rhetoric, the success of *perestroika* will depend on how effective managers in the Soviet Union can quickly learn and apply the skills of their western counterparts. In this process maybe we have something worthwhile to contribute and I suspect, in the process, we shall also learn a great deal. As the 'iron curtain' rises, maybe we can begin to exchange managerial skills and abilities along with goods and services.

As a provocative thought, if Mikhail Gorbachev or his successor called you into the Kremlin and asked your views on how to improve managerial development in the Soviet Union, what advice would you give?

# A management charter for development

A number of UK-based organizations have established a set of principles which they believe are the foundation for a management charter. The principles are fundamentally about management development. The charter has 10 points, reproduced below. What do each of the points mean to you in your job? To what extent does your organization support the charter?

---

**THE MANAGEMENT CHARTER**
*A Code of Practice for the UK*

We recognize that good management practice is essential if we are to maximize the potential of our most valuable resource: the people who work here. Their enterprise, initiative and creativity is crucial to our future success.

We are therefore committed to the following:

1  to improve leadership and management skills throughout the organization;

2  to encourage and support our managers in continuously developing management skills and leadership qualities in themselves and in those with whom they work;

3  to back this by providing a coherent framework for self-development within the context of our corporate goals, which is understood by those concerned and in which they play an active part;

4  to ensure that the development of managerial expertise is a continuous process and will be integrated with the work flow of the organization;

5  to provide ready access to the relevant learning and development opportunities—internal and external—with requisite support and time released, appropriate to our organization;

6  to encourage and help managers to acquire recognized qualifications relevant both to their personal development and to our corporate goals;

7  to participate actively in the appropriate networks of the Management Charter initiative and thereby share information, ideas, experience, expertise and resources that will prove mutually beneficial to the participants and help us to further the aims of this code;

8  directly and through networks, to strengthen our links with sources of management education to ensure that the training offered best complements our management development programmes, matching our corporate needs and future requirements;

9  to contribute to closer links with local educational establishments to promote a clear understanding of the role of management, its challenge as a career and the excellent opportunities for young people to develop professionalism in its practice;

10  to appoint a director or equivalent to oversee the fulfilment of these undertakings to review our progress annually and, after evaluating the contribution to our performance, set new targets for both individuals and the organization; and to publicize highlights from the review and the new targets.

Chief executives should undertake to communicate and demonstrate to all managers their commitment to the above code.

This is as much a political document as it is a business proposal. It identifies the importance of the managerial development process and seeks to improve its standing in the Boardroom priorities. It needs to achieve this for, despite 25 years of intensive effort in the UK, management education and development—as shown by both the Handy and Constable reports (1987)—is still in need of considerable attention.

## Management development in developing countries

The economic success or failure of the economically poorer countries in Asia, Africa and South America will depend considerably on how effectively the managers in those countries can be trained to run effective organizations. They will have to cope with local cultural problems and a low educational level among their staff. Their countries will typically have a low technology base and a high debt. They will need to educate their staff in more senses than one.

However, they will have labour at a relatively low price. They will have a large market and if they can learn quickly they could transform the living standards of their fellow men and women. This is the real test for management development.

## Management development in Japan

Japan has its own distinctive approach to management, particularly among the medium- and large-sized organizations where respect for the hierarchical leaders and traditional practices remains high.

We can learn much from the Japanese traditions and practices. Some of the key ideas, summarized below, are based on the work of Nori Suzuki (1986), who has outlined various examples and applications in his articles cited in the references. Management development is primarily done on the job, working closely with other managers. The key players and their roles are described below.

*Sempai,* literally means an 'elder' who in real terms may only have joined the company three to five years earlier but provides guidance and advice in a one to one tutorial relationship for a new employee's training. Often such tuition is conducted socially in the evenings over a drink.

*Ka-cho,* the section manager level in a Japanese organization, is a key role in the management promotion process. People who succeed usually make this role by the time they are 40 to 45 years of age. Upon becoming a *Ka-cho* a Japanese manager has, in one sense, arrived.

The normal progression in the Japanese organization, together with the names given to each level are shown in Figure 14.1, which indicates that there are three distinct stages for a Japanese businessperson in his or her career path:

1 the apprenticeship period (*Minarai—mi* means to observe, and *narai* is to learn);
2 the staff period (*Hitoridachi—hitori* means one's own and *dachi* indicates to stand); and
3 the manager period (*Kanri-shoku—kanri* means to manage, and *shoku* means the job).

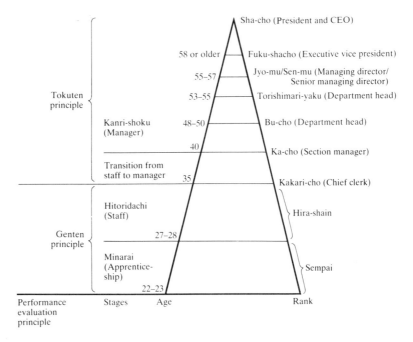

**Figure 14.1**  *Model of Japanese promotion system and evaluation standards*

Also a key difference is between the *Genten* and the *Tokuten* principles. Prior to the age of 35 the ruling principle is to master the do's and dont's and comply. However, after 35 years of age, the *Tokuten* principle is upheld where 'evaluation is based solely on the merit and contribution of the individual employee to the company'.

As Suzuki notes, 'The real irony of the situation is that many attributes recognized as necessary for the making of a good *Hira-shain* prior to age 35 turn out to be just the ones he should avoid or get rid of at the *Kakari-cho* level and beyond.

It is noteworthy that some Japanese companies are now moving to favour more of meritocratic approach particularly for the managerial levels.

## Guidelines

Management development involves both formal and informal planning and mutual learning. It is a political process of who succeeds. As I visit organizations, however, I hear managers discussing many weird and wonderful things. It is ironic, however, that one subject that is rarely high on the agenda is, 'how we manage'. It seems at times there is a conspiracy so that one manager does not learn from another.

The process of management development requires that we observe and learn from others, whether they be in the same company or from foreign countries. Therefore some guidelines you can adopt are as follows:

- Keep notes on how other managers conduct meetings.
- Ask other colleagues how they conduct negotiations or performance reviews.

- Call your team together and ask them how you manage.
- Invite your team to consider what they do well and badly and their plan for improvement.
- Write down what you feel are your managerial strengths and weaknesses and call a meeting of your team to discuss areas for improvement.

These will all have an impact on the politics of management development. Increasingly management development will be central to the issues of who gets what and why. This will be seen at national levels such as in Russia and Eastern Europe as well as at the more micro level within organizations. We can all learn a great deal from the way different cultures treat management development and transfer the best ideas to our own work.

# 15 The success factors of management development

*The trouble with most of us is that we would rather be ruined by praise than saved by criticism*

Norman Vincent Peale

## Producing relevant outputs

All activity in business should produce results. Management development is no exception. The normal criteria in private business is to see those results in quantitative form, such as improved profits reflecting increase in sales and more output for the cost of inputs. There may be other measures, such as improved safety, or a better quality product. The important thing is that there should be some measurable difference after an effective management development effort.

Too often, however, I find that management development is an act of faith. People believe that by providing good inputs there will be practical outputs. If, for example, we put down on paper a logical performance review scheme then people will, it is assumed, implement the plans. Likewise, a further assumption could be that, if we give a good lecture on a course people will take away the main points and implement them. We find too often, however, there is not too much relationship between inputs and outputs. It is for this reason that management development has to become central to the achievement of business success. It involves producing real results.

This demands an output focus. I, therefore, say to organizations before they initiate a management development activity, 'What are you trying to improve?' It is only when they can articulate what they are trying to do better, that we can discover the ways and means to do that through management development.

Management development, therefore, is a means to an end. The question is: 'What are the ends that we are pursuing?' Here are some quantifiable goals that I have developed with clients.

1 We have to generate up to 20 per cent new products in the next three to four years.
2 We need to improve our productivity by at least 30 per cent over the next two years.
3 We need to reduce absenteeism by at least 50 per cent within the next year.
4 At least 70 per cent of our managers should be promoted from within.

These are all fairly clear and quantitative objectives. They provide a basis upon which we can assess performance. In doing this, we are able to move forward with programmes that related to these specific targets.

I involve the managers in designing projects to achieve the objectives. In doing so, I enable people from different backgrounds to work together and compare ideas. I encourage them to compare their own organization with other companies in different industries. Most of all, I insist that the people work in groups and prepare action recommendations, not only for what other people should do, but what they themselves should do to improve performance in the areas mentioned.

The whole process engenders tremendous energy, excitement and enthusiasm. People recognize that the goals are real and meaningful and can improve their total organizational performance. In the process, they find that they are developing new insights, new skills and new knowledge. They learn greatly from each other and appreciate the camaraderie of the group.

This, I believe, is the future for management development. It is not just courses, or lecturers, or even performance review systems, or better compensation. It is taking a view of where the organization must go in order to succeed, and designing practical management development initiatives that will deal with these issues. In this way, people will develop as managers and simultaneously resolve key problems in the organization. That is the essence of what effective management development must be about.

## How management development can succeed

Management development can fail for any of a number of reasons. There is, however, no one factor that will lead to success. We need to consider a number of interrelated activities which, together, can bring about successful management development.

It is important, therefore, when designing management development policies, that one considers the actual behaviour that people will have to adopt, in order that the policy becomes effective. From my experience, it requires a very wide range of behaviours, which are not easy to achieve, particularly when one is trying to coordinate a large number of managers.

The essence of management development is that it does involve a co-ordinated approach, so that people in different parts of the business are doing similar things. They may do them in different ways, reflecting their own style. The important thing, however, is that they work towards some common ends and have some overall guidelines that will help them towards success.

My own work has led me to identify nine issues, which I believe are fundamental. In this chapter I have outlined these issues and given some indication of what the principles mean in practice. The chapter, therefore, sums up many earlier points and examples.

## Select high achieving managers

Too often, management development programmes are remedial efforts. They are trying to overcome basic deficiencies that should never have occurred in the first place.

The essence of successful management development is that one puts a considerable amount of effort into selecting the right people. It is far easier to develop people who are already of managerial potential than to adapt people who have little inclination, or ability, in such roles. Too often I find that management development programmes concentrate upon the latter. In essence, they are trying 'to fit round pegs into square holes'.

In real life we know that this is a situation which, on many occasions, we cannot avoid. Due to the fact that we have inherited staff that we did not select, or that the business has changed from its original small scale to a fairly large-scale operation, it is possible that we have people who must be adapted to roles for which they had not originally been selected. This is normal, and indeed any management development programme should concentrate to a certain extent upon this kind of work. We are all in the process of trying to develop beyond our own competence, and we only find out whether we can do it by trying.

The major thrust of management development should not, however, be on remedial work. It should concentrate more on developing people who have the potential to go further than the work that the organization requires.

The main objective, overall, is achievement. Unless the managers you select are high achievers, then it is unlikely the organization will go forward very fast. There are now various ways in which achievement can be measured, ranging from the work of McClelland to that of Ghiselli. The one factor that seems to be insufficiently assessed in the process of taking on new managers is *achievement*. If management development is to be effective, it is important that managers want to, and are keen to, achieve. This in itself will be a major factor in their own learning process and the way in which they manage others. At the top of my list in providing guidelines for effective management development, therefore, is the direction to select high achieving managers.

## Obtain enthusiastic managerial support

There is no doubt that if management development is to work, it must be seen as something that people regard as important. Top management must give it their support. This can range from verbal support right through to personal commitment in funding workshops, programmes, setting up special events, being involved with projects and, overall, taking management development seriously. This means going beyond setting up paper systems and other control mechanisms. It essentially means that all managers must be involved with the process and philosophy of management development.

Management development is a long-term process. It does not pay dividends overnight. It is something that involves a great deal of support and day-to-day activity. My second point, therefore, is that managers must be enthusiastic about the approach, not for a week or even a month, but continually, and in this way it will encourage others.

## Involve key people in diagnosing needs

Too often, a management development policy is agreed and a range of courses are listed for people. Unfortunately, a major step is missing in producing a successful management development effort. Managers must be involved in diagnosing their needs. If they are not, they will not be committed and will feel that they are being sent on someone else's programmes and treated very much as students rather than as adults.

When managers have been involved in the diagnosis, they have become enthusiastic supporters of any activities that emerge thereafter. Also the activities that do emerge are invariably better in quality than those that have not involved the managers at an early stage. The reason is clear. The managers know what the problems and issues are, and they are the people who can identify what needs to be done, even if they do not know how it should be done.

It is vital, therefore, that such people be brought into discussions at the earliest possible time. My own preference is that this is done through workshops and group meetings rather than questionnaires. I recognize, however, that in large organizations this is not always possible and the questionnaire needs to be used. Where this occurs, I would suggest that we use open-ended questions rather than ask people to circle numbers on scales. The latter are usually meaningless anyway, and do not provide the real data that can move management development forward.

Let us, therefore, make management development successful by bringing in the managers at the earliest stage so that they can have an input on what needs to be done, even if it is left to the management development specialist to design the learning events. Moreoever, let us not do one diagnosis but continue to re-diagnose on a regular basis, and adapt and develop the schemes so that they continually meet the client's needs. In this way we shall be customer orientated.

## Design work-related activities

Too often management development is seen as a passive, non-work-related set of activities. I strongly believe it has to be active and has to be seen to be important in terms of the jobs people do. This does not mean to say that we do not need courses. I would prefer, however, to see more workshops. I would also prefer to see workshops geared around specific problems and issues that emerge from the task of the organization, particularly those related to income, costs and productivity.

As management is a practical activity, there should be considerable opportunities for people to work on job-related problems and look at these in terms of the theories, principles and methods that have been evolved. That is to say, classroom activities need to be closely related to work activities.

My own work in this field suggests that we must lean more towards projects and specific task learning vehicles if we are to make management development successful. I have been associated with one company where classroom activities have been but a prelude for going back into the company to gather information on a project that has been set by senior management. The people work in teams of four or five. They then come back to the college environment, where they make a video film of their work on the project. This video film is then presented to the managers and forms the basis of a presentation. Such presentations have been enormously successful in influencing the way the organization at senior level begins to think about problems, and a number of video tapes have been shown widely throughout the organization. It is this link between off-the-job and on-the-job training and development that needs to be further extended.

**Press hard for outputs**

Outputs need to be very much in the forefront of anyone's mind when designing management development activities. The key question is: 'What are we going to get out of this?'

My own approach is to set time schedules and targets so that people have some indication of what is required. In this way, we are trying to make management development not only active but practical, in that it is related to outputs that are seen to be important and relevant to both the individual and the organization.

It is relatively easy to educate. It is much more difficult to manage a management development activity that has useful outputs as this requires considerable thought and affects the design of the management development activity. When setting up your next management development effort, therefore, ask yourself what are the outputs that you will ask of the people who will be involved and what effect will those outputs have upon the organization and individual performance?

**Provide early leadership experience**

It is absolutely essential that if people are to learn management, they do so by actually managing. My work with chief executives has shown that, time and time again, they learned to manage by being thrown in at the deep end. They feel that although this was a very difficult process, and one with a variety of dangers, they nevertheless learned more by having to adjust quickly. Such leadership experiences must involve the management of other people. If you are not leading others, then you have to question what indeed you are leading.

The real problems of management are those that involve coordinating and getting other people to work on tasks. People have a habit of answering back and not always doing what you think they should be doing. The learning that comes from practical leadership is therefore essential. It cannot be gained from books, although theories may help in practice.

From my research, it is also clear that people need to have experience in many functions of business prior to the age of 35. Too often accountants do not have any work experience, other than finance, until they are promoted into the general management area. Equally, engineers have considerable problems in breaking out of their professional area of specialization and, therefore, find it difficult to understand the problems of marketing, finance or indeed personnel, when they have not had experience in those areas. If we are to help people move forward, then planned experience in different functions of the business is essential.

In a recent discussion with a large company specializing in engineering products, it was stressed that anyone with the aspirations of becoming a manager required an engineering qualification. Their concern was, that there was a conflict between their recruiting policies and their senior management development policy. Upon recruitment, they selected the best engineers available. When it came to developing them as managers, however, they found that many had little interest in the managerial function and were more interested in their research specialization. In this particular case, the company had some difficulty because they did not have sufficient people with a wide understanding of the business function, beyond engineering, to deal with the vital commercial decisions that had to be made.

Management development and manpower planning must, therefore, go hand in hand. We can learn much from the army and civil service in planning 'tours of duty' for people who are being groomed for top management. People who are identified as having managerial potential should, therefore, towards the latter end of their twenties, be given planned assignments.

## Let people review themselves

This is a fundamental part of a successful review process. For too long we have had the top-down approach. In so far as managers initiate the appraisal process by writing down their views, they tend to inhibit open and genuine discussion.

It is difficult to have a realistic appraisal when you know that the manager has already written comments and is now seeking confirmation, in a discussion with you, that his or her judgement is correct. If you object, you can be seen to be causing trouble. It is very difficult to get people to change their minds once they have committed their views to paper.

Appraisals, therefore, should initially be written by the appraisees. In short, the criteria should be jointly agreed through the management development policy committee that all individuals should have the opportunity to write down how they see their performance over a period of time. This personal appraisal should then form the basis for a discussion with the manager.

At the end of the day, the manager can then write his or her own appraisal, which may well agree with the subordinate, or can add comments that disagree with the individual's appraisal. This in no way invalidates the self-review but is an alternative to which one can refer at a later date, if requested.

The important point is that, at the end of the assessment, objectives and agreements are reached about the work to be done in the next period, and these can serve as the basis for a future appraisal. The objectives should be initiated by the manager, in so far as he or she is aware of the business targets and plans to be achieved. Managers should, therefore, prepare a clear outline of requirements for the subordinates and ask how they see these requirements being achieved. It is then up to the subordinates to discuss these plans and objectives and to put forward their views on the means by which the objectives can be attained.

## Follow-up with workshops

One of the biggest contributions we can make to effective management development is to convene workshops on issues that are central to the business operation in the company. I have been involved, therefore, in establishing a number of workshops and meetings with people on issues related to how plans and targets can be achieved. These are not, however, normal business meetings, with formal agendas and a set of minutes. They are more informal, creative, open discussions, where there is a central topic and where people try to think through the next step to be taken on a collective basis. They are usually attended by people from different functions and backgrounds.

Success depends upon the extent to which people feel they can speak freely and talk about their requirements and what they will do themselves. It is sometimes valuable, therefore, to have an outsider, who has no political axe to grind, to facilitate this. In this way workshops help to reinforce what individuals have committed themselves to, but provide the support that is often necessary for teamwork.

## Make line managers accountable for management development

Too often I have noticed that management development is left to the training department. This is a recipe for disaster. Where management development has succeeded, it has essentially been integrated into the work of the line manager. Managers must plan the development of their staff and take a part in managing the process.

It is preferable, if your organization has a policy, that all key aspects of training and development must involve the line managers. When any courses are run, therefore, managers should be involved directly in doing the tuition and the follow-up work. The fact that team members see this, means that the development work has status in the organization. The fact that line managers are involved also means that they are committed, and know the problems of the people.

Management development is not something that can be delegated. It is an integral part of managing. Unless the person in a managerial position is trying to help his people learn new ways of doing the job and strengthen their professional skills, he or she is not, in my judgement, managing. The key task of a manager, therefore, is to enable the organization to function efficiently and, in the process, enable people to take on wider and more difficult tasks. This is easier said than done and what we need, increasingly, is more work devoted to helping line managers learn the skills of 'people development'.

## Guidelines

These nine points are the basis for successful management development. They are all necessary to ensure effective development and it requires skilled management by you and others to gain success.

Consider how well, on a 10-point scale, you would assess yourself and your organization on the following factors:

- Selecting high achieving managers.
- Obtaining enthusiastic managerial support.
- Involving key people in diagnosing management development needs.
- Designing work-related activities.
- Pressing hard for outputs.
- Providing early leadership experience.
- Letting people review themselves.

- Following up with workshops.
- Making line managers accountable for management development.

If any of these score less than 7 out of 10, you need to start doing something about it quickly. Between 7 and 9, you should get together everyone involved and ask them how you get to 10.

# 16 Management development policies and practices

*A man will fight harder for his interests than his rights.*

Napoleon

This chapter is an extension of the points raised in the previous ones but puts them more in a policy context. The following points can be regarded as a checklist against which you can assess the way in which management development is carried out within your own organization. If any of the issues mentioned are omitted, or not dealt with adequately, then do not expect your overall efforts to succeed.

## Clear policy and objectives

Many organizations are only now beginning to realize that they do not have an integrated view of what management development is. This is beginning to change, but still too many organizations have not established written policies that can be clearly communicated to people working in the company. The result, therefore, is a confusion in many people's minds as to what is required.

At an individual level, members of the organization have no understanding of the overall senior management's views on development and, therefore, find it difficult to plan a career. A further problem reflects itself in the work of middle and senior managers when planning new business expansion, and they find that there are insufficient people who can take on the new jobs and responsibilities.

It is, therefore, important to look at what the company's policy is on a whole range of issues affecting both the individual's and organization's performance. These will include how the company will manage the following aspects of its business:

1 Internal versus external appointments.
2 Salary and compensation benefits between different levels and functions.
3 Education and training provisions within and outside the organization.
4 The process of performance reviews across the organization.
5 Managerial philosophy underlying management promotions and career development.
6 The approach to leadership, communication and motivation throughout the organization.
7 The relation of manpower planning to corporate policy.

All the above have important implications, in terms of the jobs that people have and the way they are carried out. In practical terms, it will range from having people understand such things as how people are promoted; what educational and development opportunities exist; why outsiders are recruited; the role that graduates will be asked to play in the organization; and the managerial style, with regard to communication, that is expected. These may seem to be very general issues, but there must be a policy to cover the ambiguity that surrounds people's lives in an organization.

For most people, management development is a key issue, as it affects their own personal lives, their family, their income and style of life. It is no use, therefore, avoiding the issue. The job of senior management is to develop policies that enable people to understand their rights and obligations and to work within them, for the benefit of both the individual and the organization.

Management development will fail if there is no clear policy. People within the organization will have little understanding of the context within which they are working, or should work, in order to further their own development and that of their organization.

## Management development related to business plans

Management development is often seen as something that should be done because it is a good thing in itself. I often feel it is associated with concepts like love, trust and honesty. Everyone agrees that we should love each other, trust one's neighbour and indeed be honest; but, in reality, we all know that these are things which too often we do not do.

Management development is something with which people find it hard to disagree. It surely must be a good thing that people become more knowledgeable and more skilled. The important thing is that management development should be related to the business plans of the organization. In this way, activities will be related to the real work of the organization and there will be some criteria for measuring what is relevant. Too often the education and training plans are drawn up independently of the business plan. Indeed, it is not uncommon for the management development manager not to know the business plan before it is circulated to people throughout the organization.

It is clearly vital that if management development is to be practical and relevant, then the human resources manager should be directly involved in the business planning operation and consulted at an early stage. Only in this way can proper planning take place.

## Planned, not *ad hoc* solutions

This follows on directly from the above point, but really needs to be singled out as it has wider implications. Even, for example, when the business plans are known, there is a tendency to rush off and provide solutions without doing a thorough diagnosis of the requirements. Too often, this ends up with yet more courses, without really analysing the work requirements.

## Political issues

Management development is essentially a political activity. It involves such key decisions as promotion, the sort of appraisal report individuals receive, the reward for effort and a host of other matters. It is, therefore, impossible to separate management development from the politics of an organization. Too often, however, these matters are ignored or postponed. Management development can fail if it does not relate to what is really happening. This means that ways must be established to allow people's views and ideas to be heard in a democratic manner. I have suggested that the development organization should run alongside the normal operations organization.

## Pay and promotion

In all organizations people have some feeling for what is just. This is particularly so when it comes to who gets what in terms of rewards. Unless these are seen to be fairly distributed in relation to ability and effort, then the whole of management development is likely to be undermined, however good the systems, the courses or the processes. I have been in organizations where promotions have been announced and listened to people in corridors and offices talking about the inequity and injustice that they felt had been committed.

The clear message is that if that is the quality of the decision-making, there is little point in doing your best. It is vital, therefore, that pay and promotion are seen to be based upon output and it is, therefore, no surprise that the appraisal process has gathered momentum within the last few years.

## Management responsibilities

Management development is a line manager's job. The training department is there only to help to facilitate the provision of resources to enable managers to do their job. In my experience, however, it has too often been assumed that the training department will take over the management development work by running a few courses. On some occasions, the training department has been happy to fall into this role as it gives them an important job and increases their status.

There is, however, no escaping the fact that management development is a day-to-day issue. You do not develop people one day but not the next. As we know, people learn most from doing their job and it is the manager's task to provide the climate and structure within which people can develop. To pretend that this can be delegated is a way to abdicate. The manager must, therefore, become very skilled in coaching and devising the development of his people.

## Planned job moves

Keeping a person in a job for too long is one of the worst sins we can commit in management development. If people are to take on more demanding work, it is vital that they have experience in many functions early in their career. Most important, it is vital that they have experience of managing people. There is a danger that management development will fail because engineers are kept in engineering too long, and accountants in the finance section too long. If we are to develop senior people, it is vital that they understand the total context of the business. This is best achieved by direct involvement in various functions.

# Policy issues

I was asked by a large organization to develop some policy guidelines that would help everyone think through what they should be doing. I interviewed a number of managers and the general feeling was that the policy should concentrate more on what they regarded as the 'more personal aspects of development' within the wider structure. Following these interviews I developed a number of drafts and we eventually agreed on the guidelines shown in Figure 16.1. How does it compare with the prevailing policy in your organization? Which of the key points do you personally need to work harder upon in order to succeed?

---

### POLICY GUIDELINES

1 Management development is a key factor in increasing the standard of service to the customer and the management of the business.

2 Management development is regarded as an integral aspect of every executive's role and responsibilities.

3 Management development *primarily* involves accepting *personal responsibility* for professional development. The preparation of an annual individual development plan to achieve relevant goals will be an integral part of the scheme.

4 The organization supports management development and will, within agreed budgets, provide the opportunities for it, both at corporate and departmental levels.

5 Management development is regarded as a *long-term investment*, rather than just a short term to solve problems or fill vacancies. It should enable an executive to continue to do his or her job at a top professional level and keep up-to-date.

6 Succession from within will be the key objective and management development should be organized to foster peoples' potential for succession.

7 Management development should ensure long-term development within and between departments and a style of management where team development is facilitated and cooperation between teams is a feature of management.

8 Management development should facilitate improved sustained performance at all levels to achieve the organization's objectives.

9 It is recognized there is no one best way of management development and various options and opportunities need to be encouraged as part of a development process. Some activities may occur out of normal working hours.

---

*Figure 16.1   Management development—one organization's policy*

Any policy statement can only provide the guidelines for action. The importance of a policy lies in the involvement and commitment managers have for making it work. If your own organization does not have a policy then bring the managers together and get them to develop one. If they believe in what they are doing they will probably act to make it work. Once they own the policy they will want to own the management development that goes with it.

## Guidelines

If you concentrate on implementing the points given in this chapter, you will improve management development. Start by giving your organization a score out of 10 on each, then measure the performance in one year from now, after you have worked on the issue.

- Clear policy and objectives.
- Management development related to business plans.
- Planned, not *ad hoc* solutions.
- Political issues.
- Pay and promotion.
- Management responsibilities.
- Planned job moves.

# 17 Postscript

## Ideas for action

Finally, in what context will management development flourish? I believe we need hard rules to guide us. I have therefore drawn up some hard action-based rules to reinforce management development. The important point about these rules is that they focus an action perspective on what has to be done, with a view that it should impact upon the profitability and productivity of the business.

The 10 commandments presented in Figure 17.1 would, if rigorously enforced, have an amazing effect on the seriousness with which we take management development in our organizations. However, in most corporations I visit, the manager is making an honest and worthwhile attempt to improve performance, but with little formal backing or support. I do not know of any who have the right to impose the 10 commandments as a matter of policy. They have to make do and mend. They have to take opportunities when they are presented. Management development is therefore often a low priority.

## Summary

The 1990s will, therefore, see the acceleration of many changes in management development. The major change, however, will be the way in which we see the task before us. I believe that this will be determined far more by what I have called an existential approach. In this, managers need to see themselves as a part of the existence of those whom they wish to influence. It is about understanding through association rather than through detached analysis. It is about an involvement in the problems and opportunities. It is, however, an existential approach with a difference, in that it does involve the management developer not just taking things as they come, but having a pro-active approach and responding to real issues.

Thomas Kuhn (1970) suggested that major advances in science had little to do with scientific experimentation but more to do with the conception of a new paradigm. In essence, it requires people to look at the world in a new way, such as Copernicus did, in order that we can move forward. Only then can the process of validation have any particular meaning. I would argue the same is true in management development. We are limited by our paradigms. The time has come to review our approach and look at radical alternatives. We shall, otherwise, become the servants of our traditional conceptions of teaching and learning and not take the major opportunities that are now available.

---

### MARGERISON'S 10 COMMANDMENTS
### OF MANAGEMENT DEVELOPMENT

The Annual Management Development Plan to be agreed by the Board of Directors must reflect the following on-going principles:

1  All managers will be involved in a structured and planned process of diagnosing their own management development needs both individually and collectively in the context of the business plans.

2  No executive will be given an annual pay increase until all performance appraisals have been satisfactorily completed and subordinate staff have signed them.

3  No manager below Board of Director level should be allowed to remain in any one managerial position for more than five years without the agreement of the managing director and management development manager.

4  Every manager must be given a minimum of five days 'off-the-job' training each year against a plan they devise for themselves, and is agreed to by their manager, which is consistent with the business objectives of their unit.

5  All managers who are deemed to have 'potential' will have at least one job outside their own area of technical expertise and original functional area prior to the age of 35.

6  Managers deemed to have 'potential' will, prior to the age of 35, be given a job that has a clear profit and loss accountability.

7  All managers deemed to be promoted to the senior level just below the Board will, prior to taking up the appointment, have the opportunity to spend at least three months outside the company, preferably overseas, investigating how other companies in the same and related industries do business.

8  All managers being considered for a top appointment will also spend at least one month visiting customers and clients, and will prepare a detailed report for the Board, giving suggestions and improvements on how the visits will relate to his or her particular job when the appointment is accepted.

9  The ratio of external to internal promotions in any one year in any division must not exceed 30 per cent without the agreement of the managing director and the management development manager.

10 Each year, every manager shall write a personal logbook on 'the key learning points in my managerial work' to be submitted to his or her manager, with a copy to the management development manager, enclosing an outline plan for his or her own personal management development in the coming year as a basis for appraisal and career counselling.

---

*Figure 17.1   Action-based rules for management development*

We must look much more closely at the real demands of industry, commerce, and the public organizations. It is the challenges they have to face that should determine the forms of education and development that we produce. In essence, we have to get in touch with the political realities, as well as the commercial marketing realities.

My own approach is to try to work with groups of people in the context of organizational problems and opportunities. This is in contrast to the traditional mode of emphasizing individual development. It is not a question of whether one is right and the other is wrong. It is a question of balance and so far there has been too much emphasis on individual development. The reality of organizational life is that people have to work in groups on a customer-orientated task basis. It is here that we need more effort.

All this, I believe, indicates a much more political awareness and involvement in the real issues. It must not, however, stop there. Management development tends to be limited to those who have the designation 'manager'. We must not forget those who manage, but do not have the title. To make real progress, we need a paradigm that brings in the way we work with trade unions, who at present prefer a separate approach to the development, rarely cooperating with management initiatives for those who wish to take on shop steward or other positions.

In short, management development is fragmented and not sufficiently politically based, too product orientated, and individualistically centred. We must evolve a new paradigm that will help us tackle these issues. I believe that one way in which we can move towards this goal is to be more involved in the existence of the players on the commercial, industrial, and public pitches of managerial endeavour. I hope the ideas put forward in this book prove to be helpful to you and your colleagues.

# Bibliography

Alpander, G. Supervisory training programmes in major USA corporations. *Journal of Management Development* **5** (No. 5), 1986.

Argyris, C. *Intervention Theory and Method.* Addison Wesley, 1974.

Argyris, C. *Increasing Leadership Effectiveness.* Wiley, 1976.

Ashton, D. The trainer's role in project based management development. *Journal of European Industrial Training* **3**(3), 1974.

Ashton, D. Are the business schools good learning institutions'. *Personnel Review* **17** (No. 4), 1988.

Barnard, C. *The Function of the Executive.* Harvard University Press, 1938.

Beckhard, R. *Organisation Development.* Addison Wesley, 1969.

Bennett, R. *Improving Trainer Effectiveness.* Gower, 1988.

Bennis, W. *Leaders.* Harper and Row, 1985.

Blake, R. and Mouton, J. *The Managerial Grid.* Gulf Publishing, 1961.

Boddy, D. Some issues in the design of action learning programmes, in *Advances in Management Education* (eds J. Beck and C. Cox). Wiley, 1980.

Bolt, J. *Tailor Executive Development to Strategy.* Pergamon Press, 1988.

Bolt, J. *Executive Development.* Harper and Row, 1989.

Boyatzis, R. *The Competent Manager.* Wiley, 1982.

Boydell, T. and Pedler, M. *Management Self Development.* Gower, 1981.

Bray, D. W. *et al. Formative Years in Business.* Wiley, 1974.

Bray, D. W. Fifty years of assessment centres. *Journal of Management Development* **4** (No. 4), 1985.

Brown, M. *Richard Branson.* Headline, 1988.

Brown, W. *Explorations in Management.* Heinemann, 1960.

Burgoyne, J. Management development for the individual and the organization. *Personnel Management,* June 1988.

Butler, J. Beyond project based learning. *Journal of Management Development* **9** (No. 4), 1990.

Caie, B. Learning in style. *Journal of Management Development* **6** (No. 2), 1987.

Casey, D. Breaking the shell that encloses your understanding. *Journal of Management Development* **6** (No. 2), 1987.

Casey, D. and Pearce, D. *More Than Management Development.* Gower, 1977.

Constable, C. J. and McCormick, R. *The Making of British Managers.* CBI/BIM, 1987.

Coverdale, R. *Thought—a Framework for Teamwork.* Training Partnerships, 1968.

Cunnington, B. The process of educating and developing managers for the year 2000. *Journal of Management Development* **14** (No. 5), 1985.

Cunnington, B. and Limerick, D. The fourth blueprint. *Journal of Managerial Psychology* **2** (No. 2), 1987.

Dewey, J. *Experience and Education.* Collier Macmillan, 1963.

Drucker, P. *The Practice of Management.* Harper and Row, 1954.

Drucker, P. *The Effective Executive.* Heinemann, 1988.

Drucker, P. *The Adventures of a Bystander*. Heinemann, 1982.

Easterby-Smith, M. *Evaluation of Management Education Training and Development*. Gower, 1986.

Edwards, M. *Back from the Brink*. Bantam Books, 1983.

Espey, J. and Batchelor, P. Management by degrees. *Journal of Management Development* **6** (No. 5), 1987.

Fletcher, C. The effect of performance review on appraisal. *Journal of Management Development* **5** (No. 3), 1986.

Foy, N. Management education—current action and future trends. *Journal of European Industrial Training* (Monograph), **3**(2), 1979.

Francis, D. *Managing Your Own Career*. Fontana, 1985.

Fulmer, R. Corporate management development and education. *Journal of Management Development* **7** (No. 3), 1988.

Geneen, H. and Moscow, D. *Managing*. Doubleday, 1984.

Green, W. A. and Lazarus, H. Corporate campuses. *Journal of Management Development* **7** (No. 3), 1988.

Griffith, P. and Allen, B. Assessment centres breaking with tradition. *Journal of Management Development* **6** (No. 1), 1987.

Gorbachev, M. *Perestroika*. Collins, 1987.

Gordon, W. J. *Synectics*. Harper and Row, 1961.

Hague, H. *Executive Self Development*. Macmillan, 1974.

Hague, H. *Management Training for Real*. Context, 1979.

Handy, C. *Gods of Management*. Pan, 1979.

Handy, C. *Understanding Organizations*. Penguin, 1985.

Handy, C. *The Making of Managers*. NEDO, 1987.

Harvey-Jones, J. *Making it Happen*. Bantam, 1988.

Hersey, P. and Blanchard, K. *Management of Organization Behaviour*. Prentice-Hall, 1972.

Honey, P. and Mumford, A. *Manual of Learning Styles*. Honey, 1986.

Honey, P. and Mumford, A. *Manual of Learning Opportunities*. Honey, 1989.

Huey, J. Financial services training—the Westpac experience. *Asia Pacific International Forum* **15** (No. 3), 1989.

Hunt, J. Management development for the year 2000. *Journal of Management Development* **9** (No. 3), 1990.

Hussey, D. *Management Training and Corporate Strategy*. Pergamon Press, 1988.

Hussey, D. Executive education in the UK. *Journal of Management Development* **9** (No. 4), 1990.

Huczynski, A. *Encyclopaedia of Management Development Methods*. Gower, 1983.

Jacques, E. *The Changing Culture of the Factory*. Tavistock, 1951.

James, K. and Robertson, G. Politics and management development. Special issue of *Journal of Management Education and Development* **20** (Part 3), 1989.

Kable, J. *People, Preference and Performance*. Wiley, 1988.

Kakabadse, A. *The Politics of Management*. Gower, 1983.

Kakabadse, A. Police chief officers. *Journal of Managerial Psychology* **3** (No. 3), 1988.

Keys, B. Management games and simulations. *Journal of Management Development* **9** (No., 2), 1990.

Keys, B. and Henshall, J. *Supervision*. Wiley, 1990.

Knowles, M. *The Adult Learner*. Gulf Publishing, 1973.

Knowles, M. *The Modern Practice of Adult Education*. Cambridge, 1980.

Kolb, D. *Experiential Learning*. Prentice-Hall, 1984.

Kolb, D. Robin, I. M., and McIntyre, J. M. *Organizational Psychology: An Experiential Approach* (3rd edn). Prentice-Hall, 1979.

Kotter, J. *The General Managers*. Free Press, 1982.

Kotter, J. *The Leadership Factor*. Macmillan, 1988.

Kuhn, T. *The Structure of Scientific Revolutions* (2nd edn). University of Chicago Press, 1970.

Likert, R. *The Human Organization*. McGraw-Hill, 1967.

Livingston, J. Myth of the well educated manager. *Harvard Business Review*, January 1971.

London, M. Development for new managers. *Journal of Management Development* **2** (No. 4), 1983.

London, M. Assessment centres and management development. Special issue of *Journal of Management Development* **3** (No. 1), 1984.

London, M. and Stumpf, S. How managers make promotion decisions. *Journal of Management Development* **3** (No. 1), 1984.

Lupton, T. Business schools in the 80s and beyond. Manchester Business School and Centre for Business Research, Working Paper No. 49, 1980.

Maier, N. *Problem Solving Discussions and Conferences*. McGraw-Hill, 1983.

Mangham, I. *Management Training*. University of Bath, 1986.

Margerison, C. J. A constructive approach to appraisal. *Personnel Management*, July 1976.

Margerison, C. J. *Conversational Control Skills for Managers*. W. H. Allen, 1987.

Margerison, C. J. How chief executives succeed. *Journal of European Industrial Training* **4** (No. 5), 1980.

Margerison, C. J. Team appraisal. *Leadership and Organisation Development Journal* **4** (No. 2), 1983.

Margerison, C. J. Trends in management development. *Journal of Management Development* **7** (No. 6), 1988a.

Margerison, C. J. Action learning and excellence in management development. *Journal of Management Development* **7** (No. 5), 1988b.

Margerison, C. J. *Managerial Consulting Skills*. Gower, 1989.

Margerison, C. J. and Kakabadse, A. *How American Chief Executives Succeed*. Amacom, 1984.

Margerison, C. J. and McCann, D. *How to Improve Team Management*. MCB University Press, 1989.

Margerison, C. J. and McCann, D. *Team Management*. Mercury Books, 1990.

Margerison, C. J. and New, C. Management development by inter-company consortium. *Personnel Management*, November 1980.

Margerison, C. J. and Roden, S. *Management Development Bibliography*. MCB University Press, 1987.

Margerison, C. J. and Smeed, B. Career choices and career paths. *Human Resource Management Australia* **22** (No. 2), 1984.

Margerison, C. J. and Smith, B. *Shakespeare and Management*. MCB University Press, 1988.

Marsh, N. *et al*. Using action research to design a management development scheme. *Journal of Management Development* **3** (No. 2), 1984.

McCormack, M. *Success Secrets*. Fontana, 1989.

McQuarrie, J. *Existentialism*. Pelican Books, 1973.

Mintzberg, H. The manager's job—folklore and fact. *Harvard Business Review*, July/August 1975.

Mollander, C. *Management Development*. Chartwell Bratt, 1986.

Morris, J. Joint development activities in practice. *Journal of management development* **1** (No. 3), 1982.

Morris, J. Joint development activities: from theory to practice. Chapter 8 in *Management Development* (eds C. Cox and J. Beck) Wiley, 1984.

Morris, J. and Burgoyne, J. *Developing Resourceful Managers*. Institute of Personnel Management, 1976.

Mumford, A. *Making Experience Pay*. Gower, 1985a.

Mumford, A. (ed.) *Management Bibliographies and Reviews* **11** (No. 2), 1985b.

Mumford, A. *Handbook of Management Development.* Gower, 1986.

Mumford, A. Action learning. *Journal of Management Development* **6** (No. 2), 1987.

Mumford, A. *Developing Top Managers.* Gower, 1988.

Mumford, A. *Management Development Strategies for Action.* Institute of Personnel Management, 1989.

Newbiggin, E. Management development: panacea, placebo or punk? *The Business Graduate* **X** (II), 1980.

Pedler, M. *Self Development Bibliography.* MCB Publications, 1979.

Pedler, M. Supporting management self development., *Journal of Management Development* **1** (No. 3), 1982.

Pedler, M. *Action Learning in Practice.* Gower, 1983.

Pedler, M., Burgoyne, J. and Boydell, T. *A Manager's Guide to Self-Development.* McGraw-Hill, 1978.

Peter, L, and Hull, R. *The Peter Principle.* Bantam, 1969.

Peters, T. J. Symbols, patterns and settings: an optimistic case for getting things done. *Organizational Dynamics,* Autumn 1978.

Peters, T. J. *In Search of Excellence.* Harper and Row, 1982.

Peters, T. J. *Thriving on Chaos.* Macmillan, 1987.

Prideaux, G. and Ford, J. Management development—competencies, contracts, teams and work based learning. *Journal of Management Development* **7** (No. 1), 1988.

Randell, G. *Staff Appraisal.* IPM, 1984.

Reddin, W. *Managerial Effectiveness.* McGraw-Hill, 1970.

Revans, R. *Action Learning.* Blond and Briggs, 1980.

Revans, R. *The Origins and Growth of Action Learning.* Chartwell Bratt, 1982.

Rodgers, R. *The IBM Way.* Harper and Row, 1987.

Roskin, R. Management development—new directions. *Journal of Management Development* **6** (No. 4), 1987.

Schein, E. *Process Consultation.* Addison Wesley, 1969.

Schein, E. *Career Dynamics.* Addison Wesley, 1978.

Schein, E. *Organizational Culture and Leadership.* Jossey Bass, 1987.

Schein, E. Management education. *Journal of Management Development* **7** (No. 2), 1988.

Sculley, J. *Odyssey—Pepsi to Apple.* Fontana, 1988.

Stewart, A. and V. *Practical Performance Appraisal.* Gower, 1977.

Stewart, R. *Managers and Their Jobs.* Macmillan, 1967.

Stewart, R. *Choices for the Manager.* McGraw-Hill, 1982.

Stewart, R. Developing managers by radical job moves. *Journal of Management Development* **3** (No. 2), 1984.

Stroul, N. Whither performance appraisal? *Training and Development Journal,* November 1987.

Stuart, R. Using others to learn, in Mumford, A., *Handbook of Management Development.* Gower, 1986.

Subocz, V. Management education in Japan. *Journal of Management Development* **3** (No. 4), 1984.

Suzuki, N. Japanese MBAs. *Journal of Management Development* **3** (No. 4), 1984.

Suzuki, N. Mid career crisis in Japanese business organizations. *Journal of Management Development* **5** (No. 5), 1986.

Suzuki, N. and Skaperdas, K. The making of a Japanese manager. *Journal of Management Development* **4** (No. 2), 1985.

Tichy, N. GE at Crotonville. *The Academy Executive* **3** (No. 1), 1989.

Ulrich, D. Executive development as a competitive weapon. *Journal of Management Development* **8** (No. 5), 1989.

Vandenput, A. E. The transfer of training. *Journal of European Training* **2**(3), 1973.

Vicere, A. and Freeman, V. Executive education in major corporations,. *Journal of Management Development* **9** (No. 1), 1990.

Wieland, G. and Leigh, H. *Changing Hospitals*. Tavistock, 1971.

Wild, R. *How to Manage*. Pan, 1983.

Wills, G. Cobblers in the business schools. *The Business Graduate* **X**(II), 1980.

Wills, G. Management development through action. *Journal of Management Development* **2** (No. 1), 1983.

Wills, G. Customer first, faculty last approach to excellence. *Journal of Management Development* **5** (No. 4), 1986.

# Index

Achievement, 117
Acting positions, 65
Action learning, 37–38, 40–41
  GEC, 39–40
  MFS Chemical Company, 38–39
Adult learners, 101–102
Advisers, 48
Agenda-setting, 32–33
Appraisal, (*see* Performance appraisal)
Aquino, Corazon, 74
Arthur Andersen, 91
Ashley, Laura, 74
Assessment centres, 73
Atkinson, Sallyanne, 17
Australian Airlines, 91

Bhutto, Benazir, 74
Bolt, Jim, 99–100
Bond, Alan, 76
Boyatzis, Richard, 34
Branson, Richard, 76
Bray, D.W., 73
British and American Tobacco
  Industries, 98–99
Business schools, (*see* Corporate
  business schools, MBA courses)
Butler, Jim, 98

Career choices, 45–47
  advisers, 48
  assessing action levels, 50–51
  early job experiences, 49–50, 119–
    120
  executives, 48–49
  job changes, 63–67, 125
  objectives, 50–51
  specialists, 47–48
  supervisors, 48
Carnegie, Andrew, 76
Casey, David, 39
Colleagues, 53–55
Compensation packages, 33
  pay and promotion, 125

Competitive opportunities, 7
Constable, C.J., 112
Consultants, 7
Corporate business schools, 95
  Hamburger University and others,
    96–97
  joint development activities, 95–96
  MBA company/university joint
    ventures, 97–100
Counselling skills
  cues and clues, 78
  general comment and specific
    examples, 79
  learning from others, 81–82
  managing meetings, 82–85
  problem-and solution-centred
    approaches, 80–81
  process consultation, 79
  questions to ask, 63
  time and place, 78–79
Customer feedback, 59–60
Customer service, 7, 13

Developing countries, 112
Development centres, 73
Drucker, Peter, 49

Edwards, Sir Michael, 104
Effectiveness, 9
Eisenhower, Dwight, 104
Exchange programmes, 66
Executives, 48–49
Experience, 42–44

Feedback, 16
  customers, 59–60
Forte, Charles, 76
Franchisees, 27
Freeman, Virginia, 25

GE Company, 10
GEC, 39–40
Geneen, Harold, 72

General Foods, 99–100
General Motors, 12
Ghandi, Indira, 74
Gorbachev, Mikhail, 110
Green, W.A., 82–83

Hamburger University, 96
Handy, Charles, 112
Harvey-Jones, J., 88
Hewlett Packard, 91
High achievers, 116–117
High-fliers, 71–72
    assessment or development centres,
        73
    competition and cooperation, 74–75
    retention, 75–76
    risk-taking, 75
    The Executive Connection, 75
    women, 74
Honey, Peter, 41
Hong Kong Bank, 91
Huey, Jim, 98
Hussey, D., 97

IBM, 13, 32
ICI, 7–8
Individual development plans
    action contacts, 61–62
    agenda-setting, 32–33
    changing jobs, 63–67
    external development, 67
    job-related development, 62
    personal responsibility, 61
    self-development, 63
Induction, 13
Initiative, 71–72
Inter-company studies, 58
International Management Centres, 39
International Management Group
        (IMG), 13
International politics, 109–110
Interpersonal skills courses, 11

Japanese organizations, 57, 65, 67,
        112–113
Job changes, 63–67, 125
Jobs, Steve, 76
Joint development activities, 95–96

Kable, Jim, 100
Kakabadse, Andrew, 47
Knowles, Malcolm, 101
Kolb, D., 41
Kotter, J., 34

Kuhn, Thomas, 128

Laing, Sir Hector, 87
Lazarus, H., 82–83
Learning
    action learning, (*see* Action learning)
    adult learners, 101–102
    experience, 42–43
    from customers, 59–60
    from other managers, 53–57
    from other organizations, 57–58
    managerial learning, 41–42
    reflecting on experience, 43–44
Linking skills, 90–91, 109
London, Manuel, 49

Management charter, 111–112
Management development
    accountability of line management,
        121, 125
    action-based rules, 129
    action learning, (*see* Action learning
        assumptions, prejudices and
        hypotheses, 33)
    business responsibility, 26–29
    career choices, (*see* Career choices)
    changing jobs, 63–67, 125
    continuum, 2–3
    corporate business schools, (*see*
        Corporate business schools)
    cost effectiveness, 106
    counselling skills, (*see* Counselling
        skills)
    definition, 3–4
    developing countries, 112
    early leadership experience, 119–
        120
    entry into management from
        manufacturing or technical
        posts, 2
    executive education in major
        corporations, 25–26
    individual development, (*see*
        Individual development plans)
    involving key people in diagnosing
        needs, 117–118
    involving senior management, 12
    Japan, 112–113
    learning from customers, 59–60
    learning from other managers, 53–57
    learning from other organizations,
        57–58
    managerial requirements, 102
    mangerial support, 8–9, 117

meaningful questions, 31–32
outputs as a priority, 24–25, 115–116, 119
performance appraisal, (*see* Performance appraisal)
planning, 104–105
policy and objectives, 123–124, 126
political aspects, 106–108, 124–125
   international politics, 109–110
relevance to the business plan, 124
relevance to the corporate environment, 11
selecting high achievers, 116–117
Soviet Union, 110
structured informality, 5
terms of reference, 30
value, 24
work-related activities, 118–119
workshops, 120–121
Managerial learning, 41–42
   learning from experience, 42–43
   reflecting on experience, 43–44
Managerial roles, 68–70
Managers
   compensation packages, 33
      pay and promotion, 125
   competencies, 34
   reasons for leaving, 33–34
   senior, (*see* Senior management)
Mangham, Ian, 69
Mangold, Chuck, 75
Marks, Michael, 76
Marriott, William Sr, 85
Maxwell, Robert, 76
MBA courses, 39
   company/university joint ventures, 97–100
   value, 101
McCann, Dick, 35, 89
McCormack, Mark, 13
McDonald's, 27
   Hamburger University, 96
Meetings, 82–84, 93–94
MFS Chemical Company, 38–39
Mintzberg, H., 70
Morris, John, 95
Motivation, 13
Movers and shakers, 71–72
   assessment or development centres, 73
   competition and cooperation, 74–75
   retention, 75–76
   risk-taking, 75
   The Executive Connection, 75

women, 74
Mumford, Alan, 35, 40, 41, 43

Onassis, Aristotle, 76
Open University, 63
Outputs, 24–25, 115–116, 119
Outward-bound courses, 11

Pay, 125
Pearce, D., 39
Pedler, Mike, 40, 63
Performance appraisal, 15–16
   positive feedback, 16
   self-appraisal, 120
   team appraisal workshop, 18–23
Personal development, (*see* Individual development plans)
Peter, Laurence, 65
Planning, 104–105, 124
Political action levels, 107–108
Political planning levels, 105
Positive feedback, 16
Profit and loss experience, 26, 27
Promotion, 125
Public relations, 66–67
Presentations, 66–67
Purpose, 13

Recruitment, 12, 13
Reddin, Bill, 82
Retirement, 1
Revans, Reg, 37, 39, 40
Rewards, 13, 33, 125
Risk-taking, 8, 75
Role performance models, 50–51
Roles, 68–70
Rotations, 66
Russia, 110

Scandinavian consortium, 99
Schein, Edgar, 79
Scully, John, 75
Secondments, 65–66
Selection, 12, 13
Self-development, 63
Senior management, 12, 86, 91–93
   management by walking about, 86–87
   team development, 87–89
Shakespeare, William, 68
Shirley, Steve, 74
Sloan, Alfred, 12
Small businesses, 26–29
Smith, Barry, 68
Soviet Union, 110

Specialists, 47–48
Steering committees, 30–31
Stewart, Rosemary, 34, 64
Structured informality, 5
Supervisors, 48
Suzuki, Nori, 112, 113

Team appraisal workshop, 18–23
Team building, 16–18
    managerial linkers, 90–91, 109
    mixed level teams, 88–89
    senior management, 87–89
    team meetings, 93–94
Team management model, 89, 90
TEC (The Executive Connection), 75

Thatcher, Margaret, 74
Training, 13
Training Agency, 91

Universities, 97–100

Venture companies, 26
Vicere, Albert, 25

Weinstock, Lord, 39
Westpac Bank, 98
Wills, Gordon, 39
Women in management, 74
Workshops, 120–121